Content

Editor
Greg Payne

Design Editor
Liz Wright

Origination
Sally Robinson

Published by
Greenlight Publishing
The Publishing House, 119 Newland Street
Witham, Essex CM8 1WF
Tel: 01376 521900 **Fax:** 01376 521901
mail@greenlightpublishing.co.uk
www.greenlightpublishing.co.uk

Printed in Great Britain

ISBN 1 897738 161

Introduction

"Sorry, but I don't have anything smaller." We've all used those words on numerous occasions in our daily lives: when buying a newspaper, boarding a bus, ordering a last pint before the bar closes, or haggling over fruit and veg at a street market. It can prove an awkward moment, especially when you have nothing less that a £20 note and the vendor, conductor, barmaid or street trader has just served another customer who also had nothing less than folding money. Imagine the disappointment and frustration that would build up if the response from the other party in those situations were, "Well, I'm in the same boat. Nobody has offered the correct amount all day, so I'll have to owe you the change, or you can increase your order to a minimum of £5."

Could such a scenario occur in real life? In fact, something very similar has already happened several times, and on a massive scale, throughout Britain in the past. If you've ever seen a halved or quartered hammered silver coin you've encountered evidence of a shortage of change long before anyone thought of printing paper money. In busy markets and fairs in the reigns of monarchs such as Henry III or Edward I buyers and sellers often had only silver pence for their daily transactions. Most change consisted of fractional wedges cut from full pennies because mintages of round halfpennies and farthings never matched demand. At some periods even the scarce round fractions were halved and quartered, their small size making them very easy to lose. It resulted in the disappearance into the ground of millions of pounds worth of lost coin fragments.

Why did monarchs and their chancellors of exchequer put up with cut coins rather than minting sufficient lower values? The answer lies, to some extent, in the fact that until very recently coins were *not* tokens; a gold or silver coin could pass from buyer to seller in the fairly certain knowledge that it contained an amount of precious metal equal to its declared face value. Such was the case as late as AD 1919 when the last generally circulated English silver coins made from almost pure silver were minted. Queen Elizabeth II's coins are, in reality, all tokens. Earlier monarchs – with a few exceptions such as Henry VIII – strove to keep their coinage unadulterated if economic conditions allowed. A cut quarter might not have amounted to much in the palm of a subject's hand, but he/she could feel reasonably certain that a farthing's worth of precious metal had just passed from one owner to another.

Medieval monarchs who grudgingly issued silver halfpence and farthings never authorised quantities large enough to match increasing demand. Glance at the hammered silver pages of a Seaby's **Coins of England** catalogue and you'll find the farthings of many monarchs priced very highly to reflect their low mintages and availability to modern collectors. Apart from the cost of producing such low value coins, another harsh economic fact depressed mintage figures. The peasants feudally bound to every great medieval estate often received payments in the form of food, clothing and accommodation. It was generally assumed that such people had no need of proper money. This attitude probably caused the production and use of numerous lead tokens among the labouring classes in medieval times. They circulated locally and must also have changed hands as tallies to record stints of labour done by individual workers. Some of these leaden pieces may also have seen use as gaming counters in country districts. Enormous numbers have come to light, but very little is know about the many and varied markings found on them. It's a branch of local history crying out for further research.

Heavy disks of lead may have satisfied the needs of agricultural labourers, but bustling economic activities in towns called for something more sophisticated. That's one reason why base metal Continental imitations of English pennies found their way to Britain in early medieval times. They passed as halfpence and farthings because, as we've seen, markets cannot function without small change. Looking back even further, it seems reasonable to assume that hundreds of years earlier Celtic potin coins, made from various combinations of copper and tin, saw similar use in pre-Roman market-places. Jettons made in England in the 13th century and imported from Nuremberg and elsewhere in the 14th and much later, turn up in huge numbers on riverside foreshores and on many inland sites. Their primary function may have been as reckoning counters, then as gaming pieces; but given the desperate shortage of low denomination silver in medieval times, such attractive and well-made objects must surely have been pressed into use as small change in many local markets.

When Elizabeth I inherited England's crown the medieval world had already begun to witness tremendous changes. Enclosure of common land had thrown thousands out of employment and turned thousands more into wage earners rather than subsistence peasants. The walls of ancient towns could scarcely contain those who flocked in seeking work or their fortunes. Coal mining, metal working and other industrial activities generated wealth at an astonishing rate, while rampant consumption of all manner of goods ensured that the English were indeed well on their way to becoming a nation of shopkeepers, market traders and merchants. Wary of doing anything that might debase the coinage of her realm, yet aware of the common people's need for low denominations, Elizabeth hit on the clever idea of introducing a silver three-halfpenny and a silver three-farthing piece. Thus a customer calling at a shop or stall could buy a farthing's worth of goods and receive a three-farthing piece as change from a penny. The same applied to the customer with a two-penny piece; he/she received a three-halfpenny piece if spending one halfpence.

The last of the Tudors completed her reign without having to introduce base metal coins of the realm, although she gave a nod of approval to the copper token farthings issued by the authorities in Bristol, the nation's second largest conurbation at the time, for circulation in that city and 10 miles around. Her successor, James I, came from Scotland, where regal copper coins had been minted since the 15th century. In 1597, as James V of Scotland, he had issued copper turners. These later served as token farthings in many parts of England. A number of over-struck coins of higher denominations from other parts of the world also circulated here in the 17th and 18th centuries.

In 1613 James granted a licence to Lord Harrington for the minting of English copper farthings, at the same time issuing stern warnings that makers and users of token coinage faced heavy penalties. It must have seemed that 17th century England would never again witness privately minted money changing hands. But a great rebirth of tokens lay just around the corner.

The Civil War wrought havoc with the economy. Before and after the belligerence, neither Charles I nor the Commonwealth possessed sufficient courage or foresight to produce low denomination coins in adequate numbers to deter counterfeiters and to meet the needs of small enterprises struggling to find and retain customers in hard times. The moment had come for ordinary men and women to solve the problem for themselves. From the mid-1640s to the early 1670s perhaps as many as 20,000 tavern keepers, grocers, tobacconists, and other retailers throughout the land issued their own copper token farthings, halfpennies and (occasionally) pennies. Most pieces bore the name or initials of the tradesman, often together with his wife's initial, the nature of his business, its business address, the arms of the relevant guild or merchants' company, as well as a face value. Many town corporations joined in the free-for-all, issuing tokens, some bearing the town's coat-of-arms, for use in local workhouses and other institutions. Add mine owners, millers, apothecaries, postmasters, carriers, ferrymen and many other trades; add that octagonal, heart-shaped, square, as well as round tokens were in circulation, and you end up with an immensely rich resource for historians as well as collectors.

In 1672 the much-needed official farthings and halfpennies at last entered circulation, but it took more than two years to drive the private issues out of the economy. It will come as no surprise to read that the lessons of history went unlearned. A fresh crisis arose a century later as the Industrial Revolution flared and sparked into life. Low denomination coins were once again desperately lacking and desperately needed. Industrialists and major mining concerns stepped in during the 1790s and soon the country was once again awash with private money, this time mainly token pennies and halfpennies, the majority produced to a standard rivalling the Royal Mint's silver and gold issues. Indeed, many of the tokens were so well designed, engraved and minted they became overnight collectors' items. They usually bore the name of the firm issuing them, and an inscription on the edge often gave the places in which they could be exchanged for official money. The most attractive, usually depicting public buildings, national heroes or political events, were often sold as sets to contemporary collectors. Further shortages of official coins encouraged yet more token production in 1810-12, with silver token sixpences and shillings now added to copper pennies and halfpennies. It took the 1817 Act of Suppression prohibiting all private coinage, as well as the reintroduction of copper farthing production at the Royal Mint in 1821, to put an end to tokens.

Well, not quite. Throughout much of the 19th century workers in mining and a few other industries received payments in the form of tokens, popularly known as *truck money*, redeemable at company stores for food and other essentials. Similarly, hop-pickers in Kent were given tokens for every bushel of hops picked. These sometimes ornate pieces passed as currency in local village shops, though they were officially exchanged for legal tender at the end of the picking season.

Tokens also played their part in 19th century religious practices, as they had for centuries past. In many Scottish villages and towns possession of a communion token – given out only to the pious who attended the kirk and took communion – allowed access to the village store. Similarly the Salvation Army gave tokens that could be exchanged for soup to all who attended prayer meetings rather than sinning in gin shops.

At a commercial level High Street co-operative societies and other retailers used tokens in much the same way as modern supermarkets use plastic cards – to generate customer loyalty by giving small bonuses and discounts to those in possession of special tokens. Twentieth century token use was also restricted largely to advertising, sales promotion and toy money, with amusement arcades adding their *For Amusement Only* issues to the long story of these fascinating para-numismatic artefacts.

The following chapters discuss all and more of the token categories and token/tally-like objects mentioned above: prehistoric tallies, Mesopotamian proto-tokens, Roman lead *tesserae*, Celtic potins; early Continental base metal coins used in Britain; English and Continental jettons; British medieval lead tokens and tallies; 16th century Bristol farthings; turners and other foreign coins used in Britain or overstruck /counter-stamped for use here; 17th, 18th and 19th century private farthings, halfpennies and pennies; silver tokens of the 19th century; mining tokens, hop tokens, communion tokens and similar religious issues, toy money; Victorian advertising tokens; co-op tokens; and workhouse and institutional tokens.

There is no universally accepted agreement on what is/is not a token, nor even a tally. In this book the terms *token* and *tally* mainly cover those metal objects for which there is some historical or archaeological evidence that they served either as substitutes for denominations of legal money in short supply, or as a means of recording promised payments and services due, or as a method of keeping account of time, of possessions, of work output, or of the many other things humans felt a need to count and record. The accompanying texts and illustrations serve as an introduction to each category. The recommended bibliographies and the dealers' listings should put readers on the road to expertise in all of these fascinating series.

Many people have assisted with photographs and advice during the research stages of this book, and I am especially grateful to the experts whose details you will find in the dealers and specialist collectors listings.

Acknowledgements

An author's name beneath a book's title can be likened to a colourful bloom at a horticultural show: it attracts attention by deflecting the reader's eye and thoughts from the stem, leaves, roots, surrounding soil, the miracle of photosynthesis, and the toils of the gardener who transformed the seed into a potential prize winner. Something similar usually happens in the world of books, so let me deflect the admiration from the cover and acknowledge those who put in at least as much effort as mine to get this book into your hands.

First, I acknowledge my debt to publisher, Alan Golbourn, without whom this book would not be in print. Also, to Editor Greg Payne for double-double checking all that I had double checked at manuscript stage and still missed a few typos and other errors. Dan Golbourn and Liz Wright deserve special acknowledgement for their efforts at the crucial layout and design stages in the production of a book that depends heavily on the eye appeal of its pages. Others at Greenlight Publishing, notably Bryan Oram, did some sterling back-room research work to ease my burdens.

Now let me acknowledge the enormous help given by those dealers and specialist collectors who responded positively to my requests for help with material for illustrations. I do not exaggerate in declaring that without their generous assistance this book could not have been published. So thanks once again, in alphabetical order, to:-

Andy Agauthier, for Transatlantic co-operation

Gordon Bailey, who provided expert help on and images of early jettons and other tokens

Sue Bradshaw, for some excellent images of medieval leaden pieces

Ivan Buck, for early medieval expertise and images

Noel and Alan Cox, for a mountain of Welsh authority

John Gough, an amateur historian with a professional's presentation skills

Gill Hawkins, a very helpful museum manager

David and Georgina Magnay, brimming with knowledge about toy money, spade guineas and more

Alan Milne, the man to ask when it comes to questions about Scottish communion tokens

Peter Morris, for a wealth of token, check and tally images from every age

Jennie the Pedlar, for more lovely leaden images

Chris Rudd, an authority on Celtic money

Robert Sharman, a numismatist and specialist in tokens

Mark Smith, a dedicated expert on mining and associated paranumismatica

David Stuart, for a fund of 17th century token images

Paul Withers, a source of books and more on every aspect of this wide-ranging subject

Finally, a very special acknowledgement to those who helped but failed to get a mention above. They are missing due only to my incompetence.

Ted Fletcher

Chapter 1

Ancient Tallies & Tokens

Writing in 800 BC, the Greek poet Homer retold the myth of Polyphemus, a Cyclops, blinded in his solitary eye by Odysseus and his men during their attempts to escape from the giant's cave. To count his flock of sheep each morning, sightless Polyphemus had to use a system familiar to every Ancient Greek herdsman and still practised in some parts of the world today: he allowed each animal to pass through a narrow gate, then he dropped a pebble into a bowl to record its passage. Asked later how many sheep he owned, the blind giant held up his bowl and said, "This many."

The story Homer set down offers one of the earliest literary examples of one-to-one numerical correspondence. The blind giant did not need to know any words for numbers save the number one. His method provides an example of pre-number counting.

Thirty thousand years earlier, a Neolithic human used a flint blade to score groups of five lines on a fragment of wolf bone found recently by archaeologists in Slovakia. Perhaps this prehistoric record-keeper wished to remind himself of the number of wolves he had killed while protecting his family. Another ancient bone, from a baboon's leg in this case, turned up in an African cave. It bore 29 notches, interpreted by some archaeologists as a primitive calendar. But nobody can say for certain because piles of pebbles and pieces of incised bone are tallies. They provide numerical records, but they don't tell us what is being counted. The tallies can be used again and again to record the same number of something totally different. Jump forward in time to a modern fieldwalker making his way across a ploughed field. He discovers a lead disc embossed with several parallel lines. An interesting find; but until the fieldwalker learns more about the artefact and any additional meaning its markings might have, the lead disc can only be called a tally.

Another convenient way to record a tally is to take a piece of wood, split it, then score marks across the two edges formed by the break. Every piece of wood splits in a unique manner, so each notched pair of tally sticks provides a virtually forgery-proof record. Little wonder that tally sticks have proved popular for thousands of years in institutions where accounts of debts, rents, fines and dues require safe storage. The English Royal Exchequer kept its accounts with tally sticks from the 12th to the 19th

Tally inscribed on a fragment of bone. It provides a permanent record (unless an animal gnaws the bone) but we have no way of knowing what was being counted.

Tally inscribed on a split stick. Thanks to the unique splitting lines, tally sticks are proof against forgery. Nor can they be falsified unless both parts of the tally are aligned. Sticks like this set the Houses of Parliament's records archive ablaze in 1834.

century, for the sensible reason that when compared to parchment, wooden sticks suffered far less damage from rats and dampness. When the tally system finally gave way to paper records in 1834, tellers in the House of Lords had to dispose of thousands of sticks. They decided to use them as fuel for boilers in the basements, but the fires soon got out of control. Both the Palace of Westminster and the Houses of Parliament went up in flames.

More than 10,000 years ago, nomadic herding communities living in what we now call the Near East also used tallies. They had already discovered the technique of firing clay to make pots, so making small clay cones and other simple shapes required no major innovation. I can think of one clear advantage of a cone over a round pebble: the cone stays put, and a batch of cones would be less likely to mix inadvertently with another batch when standing on their flat ends. These artefacts, found on many ancient sites in the region, seem to have functioned as tallies. If a man wished to record that he had 20 ewes in his flock he needed 20 tallies. But he could use the same tallies many times over to record other information at a later date.

Somewhere in Mesopotamia around 8,000 BC – a time when the world's first farmers and village dwellers had recently turned their backs on nomadic hand-to-mouth existence – there came a staggering breakthrough in human communications. It occurred to one sharp human brain that if blobs of clay were moulded into different shapes, one shape could mean sheep, for example, while another shape might represent sacks of barley. At first these new types of tallies still had a one-to-one relationship with whatever they represented. Then came a second breakthrough: the idea of marking one tally with one or more incisions using a wedge-shaped stick. In that way a piece of clay moulded to the approximate shape of a sack and incised with five cuts immediately took on the symbolic, or *token* meaning: *this object represents five sacks of barley.* The shape and the markings on the token now carried its meaning. Only a relatively short step was needed from that concept to the invention of other wedge-shaped marks that came to mean such useful phrases as *belongs to… given by… bought from…* and more. Cuneiform writing

Simple cone-shaped clay tokens that could stand on their flat ends were an improvement on Polyphemus' pebbles.

was just around the corner, although it took several thousand years to develop and to spawn Ancient Egyptian, Greek and Latin. The use of tokens continued in all of those civilizations, but note that the Mesopotamians had an abundance of clay, thanks to their propensity for digging irrigation ditches. The Egyptians possessed an abundance of reeds along the banks of the Nile, which they used to make papyrus, a material not best suited for tokens. I would argue that this is one factor worthy of consideration when seeking reasons for fewer ceramic tokens left for us to admire once the Mesopotamian culture was overthrown.

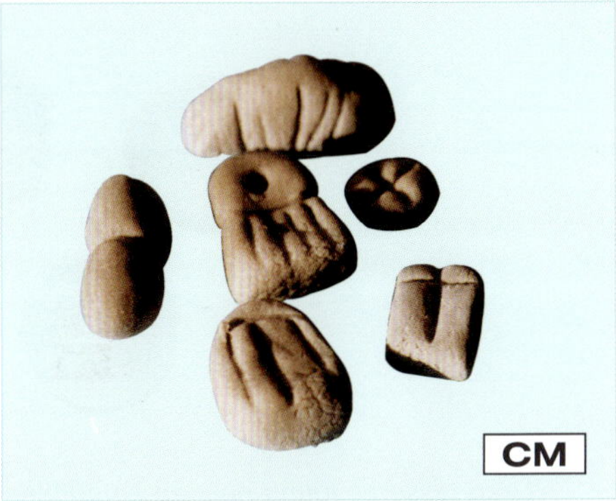

Complex clay tokens, each incised with a tally, were an important innovation in Mesopotamian culture 8,000 years ago. Records of different possessions – sheep, jars of oil, measures of barley, for example – could now be kept together without confusion. Baking to harden the clay provided a permanent tally. Bureaucracy was born.

Meanwhile, as social life in the Near East became more complex, so did the use of tokens and the inscriptions and other marks made upon them. In the region of Sumer, for example, clay cones, cubes, triangles, spheres, discs, zoomorphic and other shapes were moulded to represent jars of oil, bales of cloth, farm animals, loaves of bread, pots of alcoholic beverage, ropes, mats, perfumes, metal tools and more. Five hundred distinct shapes have so far been identified. The Sumerians seem to have required these objects for every aspect of their daily lives. Yet despite the plethora of tokens, the use of simple tallies never died out, especially among rural rather than urban populations.

It took until the 1st millennium BC for humanity to progress to money. Credit for the invention is usually assigned to the Lydians, a group of people occupying land to the north of what had been Sumer thousands of years earlier. The Lydians must have come into contact with tokens, so perhaps we should say that coins derived from tokens. The Lydian innovations lay in standardising the weights of small metal flans, impressing them with designs denoting regal authority, and guaranteeing their intrinsic value. As to raw material for making them, the gravels of nearby mountain streams held an abundance of ore that yielded electrum (a naturally occurring alloy of gold and silver) when smelted. Copied by the Greeks, then the Romans, coinage - as we understand the term today - had begun. But tokens thrived alongside the electrum, gold, silver and other official money.

For example, archaeologists digging in Greece have found numerous tokens made from bone, terracotta, lead and bronze that seem to have been used as tickets of admission to official functions, religious ceremonies and other gatherings. Dozens of lead tokens on display in an Athens museum date from the 4th century BC, and are decorated with images including bows and arrows, cows, dolphins, and crossed torches, as well as lettering. They have been interpreted as safeguards against loss of pay issued to poorer citizens who had to attend court on official business. An excavation at the ancient Greek site of Kamarina uncovered 150 lead tokens bearing

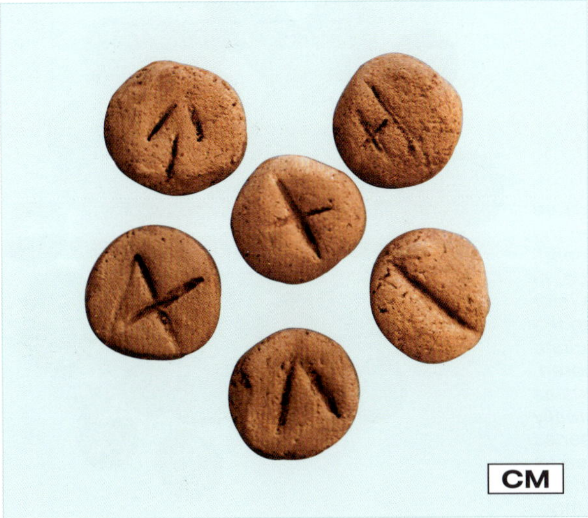

Clay gaming tokens from Roman Egypt; 2nd century AD. Provided that players agreed beforehand on how much each incised or impressed mark represented in money, a variety of games could be played with small tokens like these. And money could change hands simply by passing the token from one player to another.

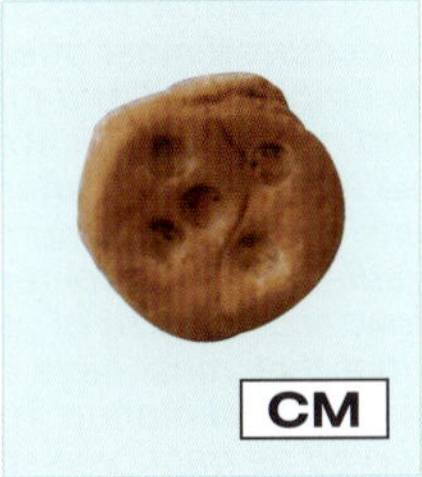

Lead tesserae found near an amphitheatre in Roman Egypt; 2nd century AD. They are engraved with what might be zodiac signs – Pisces, Capricorn, Taurus.

Two of the zodiac (?) tesserae are uniface, but one has engraving on both faces, as shown here.

citizens' names. They seem to have been issued as lottery tickets to men hoping to win election to municipal office. And in the British Museum there are some small lead tokens bearing images of comedy and tragedy masks. They date from the 3rd century BC and were probably used as entrance tickets to Greek theatres.

The Romans used the word *tesserae* to refer to tokens of bone, ceramic, lead and bronze. These tesserae circulated throughout the Roman world, nowhere more prolifically than in Rome itself where hundreds of thousands of plebeians and other free but impoverished citizens benefited daily from bread handouts. No emperor dared to end the custom and risk the wrath of the mob, but possession of a bread token was always part of the social contract. Tacitus referred to the policy as "bread and circuses". Excavations on the site of the Circus Maximus confirm that lead and bronze *tesserae* were just as commonplace in the Roman circus industry – as entrance tickets to the games, as brothel tokens, as receipts for issues of weapons to gladiators, and as part of the massive gambling frenzy that gripped the entire city when gladiators engaged in mortal combat.

Following the deaths of Anthony and Cleopatra, Egypt became the jewel in the Roman crown, famed for its wealth and agricultural yields. One way to gain maximum profits from these resources, including the grain needed to feed Rome's poor, was to ban the use of Roman coinage in Egypt. Instead a series of token coins in billon, bronze and lead, unacceptable elsewhere in the Empire, were minted and used to pay for Egyptian produce. Roman silver coins did not circulate in Egypt for more than 200 years after its annexation; all profits coming out of Egypt went directly to the Emperor. The authorised tokens often bear images of Egyptian gods, such as Isis, or personifications of the Nile, or crocodiles; but most obverses carry a portrait of a Roman emperor or members of his family.

Whenever production of Roman coins from official mints, either in Britain or on the Continent, failed to match British demand, counterfeits inevitably took their place. In Britain this occurred most often in the later years of the Empire, and at a time when the emperor depicted on many coins wore a radiate crown. Because legends were often blundered, the coins are known to numismatists as barbarous radiates. Silver content eventually became so low, and the size of the forgeries so small, that they must have circulated as mere tokens of official money. They probably also served as fractional small change.

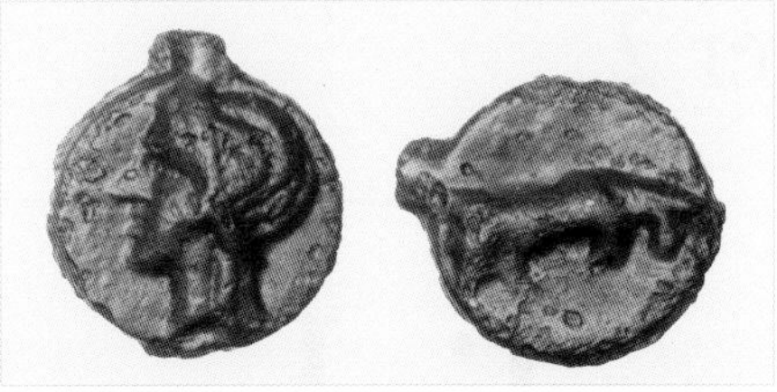

Celtic potin from Britain; 1st century BC; found in Kent. Celtic gold and silver coins had values too high for small purchases in local markets. A token coinage made from copper/tin/lead alloy served everyday needs.

Later British potin; 1st century BC; found in Essex. Flatter and lighter, this new type required less metal when cast. Sprues from the casting process remain on many specimens, as here. The stylised design required only a few strokes. These tokens could be manufactured quickly by local smiths to meet local needs.

The Empire's economy had declined to a much poorer state a few centuries later when Rome's enemies pressed hard against the frontiers and repeated debasement of silver currency was the only means of balancing the books. In Britain, imitation coins with blundered inscriptions and ever decreasing size circulated as tokens of earlier *antoninianii*. Known as *barbarous radiates* from the radiate crown worn by the ruler of the obverse, they shrank to barely 5mm diameter and are often referred to as *minims* or *minimissimi*. However, they were not Britain's first experience of token coinage. Before the Romans arrived Celtic tribes here and on the Continent produced superb gold and silver coins based on the gold staters of Philip of Macedon, and silver *drachms* of Alexander the Great. But such high value coins could not satisfy the needs of common people who had to make day-to-day purchases in local market places. Potin (the French word for pewter) answered that need. Potin coins have come to light in their thousands on numerous Celtic sites. They do not seem to have been produced to any universally accepted weight standard; even within one tribe or tribal type there are many variations. They circulated as token coinage, accepted by general consensus as a medium of exchange, in the same way as we use paper money today.

In Britain the earliest variety was the Thurrock potin, found throughout eastern Kent. The first issues depicted a reasonably accurate head of Apollo on the obverse and a butting bull on the reverse. But the design soon deteriorated to little more than a blob on each side as a result of mass production. At some point - perhaps early in the 1st century BC - the Thurrock potin gave way to a new style of flatter and lighter coin, with a stylised design depicting the head and the bull in a few quickly scribed lines. These tokens were produced by a moulding process that often left a sprue attached to the finished piece.

I have attempted to demonstrate in this fleeting survey of prehistoric and early historic times that long before England existed as a state the uses to which tallies and tokens had already been put – as accounting records, receipts, emergency and imitation money, tickets and gaming pieces – foreshadowed their use in almost identical ways nearly 2,000 years later in 17th,18th, 19th and 20th century Britain. As we shall see in the next chapter, it was imitation money flooding into the country that gave the authorities their first problems with tokens.

Identifying Finds In The Field

Fieldwalkers and excavators should examine any finds of lead, bronze or ceramic fragments for signs of deliberate marking or scoring that might indicate use as ancient tallies. Celtic potins with their stylised markings and often rich black patina are unmistakable. On late Roman sites the majority of coin finds will be token issues. The smaller their diameters, the more likely that they are imitation money.

Recommended Further Reading

Before Writing Vol. 2: **A Catalog of Near Eastern Tokens** by Schmandt-Besserat D., University of Texas Press, Austin, Texas, 1992.

Tetradrachms Of Roman Egypt. Lead Egypto-Roman Token Coinage and Currency of Egypt in the 5th Century. J.W. Curtis, 1990.

Chapter 2

Early English Tokens & Imitations

In his fascinating book **A History Of Money**, Glynn Davies points out that money-less societies frequently use cattle and other livestock as coinage, and that the Celtic Welsh economy seems to have followed that model until partial conquest by Anglo-Normans in the 13th century exposed Welsh sheep breeders to English markets and long-cross pennies.

Something similar occurred in the early Anglo-Saxon world where wealth on the hoof replaced Roman money for about 100 years until trading contacts with the Continent around AD 600 brought a few Merovingian gold tremisses to these shores. By AD 630 Anglo-Saxon rulers were minting native gold thymsas, and by AD 680 silver sceattas had begun to circulate in the south. But we must look northward to the kingdom of Northumbria for the first examples of what might have been English tokens.

Northern rulers began their metallic coinage around AD 680 with silver sceattas bearing the king's name and depicting mythical beasts on their reverses. By AD 800 the local northern economy had declined as a result of wars, and with it the coinage, which suffered gradual debasement. By AD 860 most Northumbrian sceattas were silver-less, being struck from copper and brass, though they retained some outward similarity to the earlier silver issues.

My limited experience of finding these coins occurred many years ago on the promontory not far from Whitby Abbey in North Yorkshire. A huge Anglo-Saxon market regularly took place in the vicinity of the abbey, attracting traders from all parts of Britain. Southern silver sceattas and northern debased sceattas, as well as copper and brass styccas (as they are often known) came to light together in this trading context. I wonder now if the styccas served as token fractions of the southern sceattas in a busy market context where small change must have been in demand. To use copper and brass in that manner would have required not only agreement within the marketplace on what each piece was worth in relation to the silver coins, but also some local authority to guarantee that anyone who accepted styccas could exchange them later for silver coins at the agreed rate. If that's what happened then it's as near as damn it to how 17th century token farthings functioned in the marketplace almost a thousand years later.

With the Anglo-Saxon example in mind, let us now move forward in time a few hundred years to the more diverse economies of early medieval Europe. This was the dawning of the age of mercantilism, when international trade expanded and marketplaces became the focal points of many cities and towns. Never before had there been a more pressing need for money of all units and fractions; but it was as ingots that much wealth found its way to our islands in the 13th century. The discovery of rich silver mines in central Europe led to huge amounts of bullion flowing into England in exchange for wool and other exports. Much of the silver returned to the Continent in the form of English short-cross pennies, used to pay for luxury goods, and also as bribes to allies who supported the English crown in its various disputes with the French monarchy. Because of their sterling silver content (0.925 fine) English pennies were regarded as trustworthy money and rarely went into the melting pot; instead they circulated at their correct face value vis-à-vis local money in the Low Countries, in Germany, and, in fact, wherever debased native coins were not trusted. But the English short-cross penny had one serious disadvantage: the ease with which its edges could be clipped without cutting into the central cross.

This is a modern struck reproduction of a groat for Bigbury. It is a rosette mascle issue of Henry VI and was struck to special order. What a pity that no coins were struck of Bigbury!

A Henry VI groat of Calais. It carries a mascle after "REX" but is otherwise unidentifiable. (Ex-Seaby's Black Museum).

A Henry VI groat of the London mint, ex-Seaby 's Black Museum.

A Henry VI halfpenny of the trefoil issue, again from Seaby's Black Museum.

An Edward IV first reign heavy coinage groat.

These pieces (left), used in Ireland, were prepared by cutting down to the inner circle on the penny and the half groat.

In 1247 new coins with a cross that extended from edge-to-edge began to pour from mints in England as Henry III attempted to defeat the clipping fraudsters. Inevitably these long-cross pennies became enormously popular on the Continent, to the extent that the anti-clipping design was widely imitated on local currencies. This was not necessarily with deception in mind, but often to indicate similarity and therefore trustworthiness. Medieval coins from adjacent or nearby kingdoms often exhibited similar designs; the consistency may have given the populace some assurance that the coins in question were accepted in more than one kingdom or principality.

Financial authorities in our present age of paper money have a complex range of controls they can apply to balance the nation's books – interest rate hikes, direct and indirect taxation, public investment, and more. Medieval monarchs had simpler tools: decrease/increase the silver content of coins; decrease/increase the size/weight of coins; or outlaw the export/import of coins. Rarely did two monarchs adopt the same measures at the same time, and if the price of silver in one country was low its coins would, irrespective of import/export bans, be drawn to countries where they could be melted and re-coined at a profit. (Economists refer to this as "Gresham's Law": the tendency for money of lower intrinsic value to circulate more freely than money of higher intrinsic value and equal nominal value. Non-economists say, "Bad money drives out good.")

Consider, for example, what happened in the reign of Edward I (1272-1307) who succeeded his father while crusading in the Holy Land. As the new king made his way homeward he concluded an important wool trading treaty in the Low Countries, which gave an invigorating spurt to foreign coins coming into England. He also acknowledged the need for larger and smaller coin denominations to benefit trade, and he wanted to tackle the problem of counterfeiting and underweight foreign imitations. In response to all these pressures, Edward introduced completely new coins in 1279. They included multiple, whole and - more importantly - fractional pence: groats, pennies, halfpence and farthings. Millions of coins were struck at London and Canterbury where the public could take their old, underweight, short and long-cross pennies to the mints and exchange them for new coins of the correct weight and fineness. As in previous reigns, the new English coins were much admired on the Continent and extensively copied there, some in poorer silver. However, this only made Edward's coins more popular and severely drained the home supply of silver. As a result the export of English coins was forbidden in 1299; but that did not prevent circulation of the pre-1279 English pennies on the Continent where the design was often imitated.

Some Continental rulers also imitated the newest English coins, often striking them in good weights and fineness, and sometimes with the same lettering. It is these to which the term "esterlings" is often applied. They were not intended to fool foreign merchants, and should not be confused with esterlings of lower silver content and lighter weights that created problems when they passed in trade to England. Careful checking with coin weights, tumbrels or penny poizes often took place when such money was offered, with a trusted foreigner on hand to help settle disputes and perhaps reach agreement on exchange rates for unfamiliar coins.

It is largely light or debased issues, which are referred to as crockards, pollards, rosaries, brown sterlings, lushburgs, etc. Here's what the **Oxford English Dictionary** tells us about some of these long-forgotten words:-

crockard: A kind of foreign money, decried as base under Edward I. (Citations: "Bad monies which are called crokardz" (AD 1300); King Edward damned suddenly false money that was slyly brought up. Men called this money crocards. (1387 AD); Afterwards crockards were cried down to a halfpenny. (AD 1605)

pollard: from a dialect word meaning "head", in reference to [that] device [on the coin]; (Citations: "They put forth pollards little by little and privately in stead of sterlyges. [The King] made one of them worth an half peny." (AD 1387); "There was a considerable circulation of Flemish coins, apparently of low purity, called pollards, crockards, scaldings, brabants, eagles, leonines, brown sterlings, etc." (AD 1866)

rosary: A base or counterfeit coin, of foreign origin, current in England during the 13th century at the value of a penny. (Citation "These foreign coins, called mitres, lionines, rosaries, etc., from the stamp or figure impressed upon them, were privately brought from beyond the seas and uttered here for pennies." (AD 1749)

lushburg: A base coin made in imitation of the sterling or silver penny and imported from Luxemburg in the reign of Edward III.

It may surprise some readers to hear of so many different coins circulating in 13th century England, a country renowned for its sterling pennies; but that was, in my view, one of the main reasons why these foreigners circulated: because fractions of sterling pennies were either in short supply or non-existent. Neither English nor Continental monarch ever grappled successfully with this problem of small change.

Sterling Imitations Of Edwardian Type

These are sometimes known as "Lusshebournes" because many of them come from Luxemburg from which the name is derived.
In the late 13th century, from circa 1280, vast numbers of imitation sterlings were produced on the Continent, mostly in the Low Countries. These pieces were used for trade and are plentiful in English hoards.
They are usually put into one of several categories:-

Crockards - are those with a chaplet of roses across the forehead instead of a crown

Pollards - have a bare headed bust.

The vast majority do have a crown, which makes them more difficult to identify and in all cases it is necessary to read the legends to allocate them to where they were struck and for whom they were prepared.

CM

CM

CM

CM

CM

CM

CM

CM

Sterling Imitations Of Edwardian Type

CM

CM

CM

CM

CM

CM

CM

CM

Here, for example, is a list of silver coins, and their value in English pence, likely to have changed hands in one Low Countries marketplace in the late 13th century:-

gros tournois = 3 new English pennies
ridder (depicts a cavalier) = 2 old English (pre-1279) pennies
flyoger (depicts an eagle) = 2 old English pennies
English penny = at face value
Westphalian penny = three-quarters of a new English penny
halling = half of an old English penny
lonsche = third of a new English penny
kopkiin = fifth of a new English penny.

A closer look at the **OED** citations raises some interesting points. I wonder how "brown sterlings" fooled anybody, if that claim is made by those who would doubt my contention that they probably functioned as token coinage. Their very colour, presumably a result of base metal content, rendered them obviously different and instantly recognizable; surely not the intentions of a cheat trying to pass them off as other than what they were?

The phrase "King Edward damned suddenly ..." actually confirms an ancient law that gave the monarch authority to declare *any* foreign coins to be legal tender when it suited his needs. If the king acted suddenly against crockards, I would argue that crockards may have been in English circulation before that sudden moment. Perhaps Edward had one eye on the commission he received on all newly minted coins. The removal of crockards would have required the minting of sterling pennies to replace them.

The sentence "The King made one [pollard] worth half a peny." clearly indicates that pollards were already in general use in England, perhaps at different and locally agreed exchange rates in different marketplaces. Large numbers must have contained silver worth slightly more than half a penny because it is reported that the immediate effect of Edward's decree was a flood of pollards back to the Continent, where they would have been melted down and re-coined according to Edward's valuation.

This brief glance at the situation with regard to imitations and possible tokens in the mid-13th century is mirrored in later centuries. Indeed, the reluctance of monarchs or governments to mint fractional coins with a nominal value lower than their intrinsic value, and to guarantee that they would be exchanged for whole units, was never tackled in medieval times, nor, as we shall see in later chapters, in any period down to very recent times.

Identifying Finds In The Field

Any site or fieldwalking survey that produces hammered coinage featured in Seaby's **Coins of England** is likely to hold examples of the crockards, pollards and other fascinating pieces discussed above. Many readers will possess sufficient knowledge to spot such clues as blundered inscriptions, lightness of weight and incorrect size; but their knowledge was hard won during years of involvement with the subject. If in doubt or inexperienced, show your hammered coinage finds to such experts. Don't allow anyone to dismiss your discoveries as "mere fakes, forgeries, or crockards". Look upon them as fascinating finds worthy of space in any collection that seeks to reflect everyday social conditions in medieval England.

Recommended Further Reading

History Of Money by Davies G.; University Of Wales Press, 2002.
Making A Living In The Middle Ages by Dyer C., Penguin Economic History Series, 2003.
Medieval English Groats, by Buck, I., Greenlight Publishing.

Chapter 3

Medieval Jettons

Let me start by clearing up a spelling confusion. The preferred **Oxford English Dictionary** English spelling is jetton; the French use *jeton*; the Belgians, who once produced huge quantities of these pieces, say *leggelt*; while the Germans call them *rechnen pfennig*.

We are all referring to coin-like brass counters formerly used in conjunction with a chequered board to figure and balance accounts. They date from a pre-calculator age when many people were phenomenally quick and accurate at mental arithmetic, though I'm pleased to say that no knowledge of mathematics is required to appreciate them as collectors' items today. Fieldwalkers and medieval/post-medieval archaeologists turn them up in surprisingly large numbers. For example, in 1996 archaeologists carried out an emergency dig on a medieval occupation site at Mill Lane, Thetford, Norfolk in advance of housing development. Small finds included 23 coins, 3 tokens and no less than 37 jettons. Furthermore, whenever excavations take place on ecclesiastical sites such as monasteries and abbeys, jetton finds often run to hundreds. Indeed, an old name for jettons is "abbey pieces", either in reference to their proliferation on such digs, or with an eye to the biblical or religious quotations engraved on some jettons.

They first appeared in England in the reign of Edward I (1272–1307) and the obverse images look so much like those on sterling pennies, with a facing crowned bust of the monarch, we have to assume that regal coin engravers had a hand or two in their production. Most authorities state that the easiest way to recognize an English jetton of that period, and to avoid confusion with similar French jettons of the age, is to look for a centrally pierced hole in the English piece. Piercing is said to have been necessary to prevent fraudulent passing of a jetton as an English coin. This strikes me as a rather unsatisfactory reason for poking a disfiguring hole through an attractive possession. After all, brass must have been easy to distinguish from bright silver. A more plausible explanation might be that because large numbers of debased foreign crockards, pollards and the like circulated freely as fractional pennies, there was a danger that debased silver and dull brass looked too much alike in a busy marketplace. Whatever the reason for it, piercing or indenting the centres of jettons went on in all reigns up to Richard II.

If piercing or indenting occurs on most medieval English jettons, in what other ways can we identify the early ones of Edward I's reign? Well, almost all Edward I jettons depict the monarch's head; the reverse is very often a long fleur-de-lys flanked by a star and crescent moon, a favourite Plantagenet devise. The borders of these jettons usually include rosettes on obverse and reverse faces. There are no legends, and the jettons are small in comparison to later types. If the monarch's crown has three flowering points, the jetton almost certainly dates from the early years of Edward I. Jettons from this reign only changed to a crown with two flowering points during the last five years of the kingship.

Edward I's long reign coincided with years when numerous crockards flooded into England. The monarch's crown on the crockards has three small bunches of roses, which distinguish it from the true sterling with its three-point crown. Jettons based on the crockard, with a similar rosy crown, also circulated at this time. Some have an obverse depicting a counting board, a design that appears on no other jetton of the period. When examining the crowns on early jettons, especially if from ecclesiastical sites, you may spot the crown replaced by a bishop's mitre. This is a strong indication of a jetton struck for use by monks working on Church accounts.

Medieval English Jettons

*English jetton of Edward I.
Obverse sterling head.
Reverse star and crescent.*

English jetton of Edward I. The obverse shows a sterling head. The reverse design is a long cross with six pellets in each quarter.

English jetton of Edward II the reverse showing a long cross with three pellets in each quarter.

Obverse and reverse of English medieval jetton.

English jetton of Charles II. The obverse shows a bust of the monarch, the reverse the royal coat of arms.

Obverse and reverse of English short cross jetton of Edward I, with single pellet in each quarter.

English jetton of Edward II the reverse showing a three-armed cross with pellets.

English jetton, the obverse showing three fleur-de-lys within a shield. The reverse design is a cross of three strands fleuronee with a quatrefoil in the centre.

English medieval jetton.

English jettons 13th-15th century.
as shown in an 18th century pamphlet

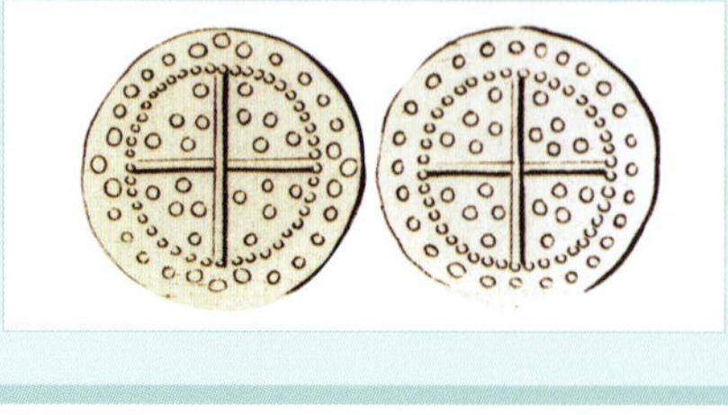

Not to scale

When Edward II came to the throne in 1307 some changes occurred in jetton designs. Generally there was an increase in diameters compared to jettons of the previous reign. The monarch's crown also changed from a three to a two-pointed design. The use of jettons became much more widespread, and there is evidence from marketplace finds of their circulation as small change in many parts of the country. Large numbers of imitations of the larger types soon flooded in from the Continent to meet popular demand for small change. The reverses altered quite a lot in this reign, though the standard obverse kept faith with the sterling. New reverses included three-armed crosses, keys and lions. Obverses often include stars and crescents. On jettons of this reign that do not carry a portrait, the commonest designs are heraldic lions, eagles on shields, lamb-and-flag emblems, and double-headed eagles. Increasing numbers of imitations, some crudely made, appeared around this time.

Edward III's reign (1327-1377) witnessed completely new types of counters: larger, thicker, with legends (*Garde Robe Regis*) and a portrait of the king standing beneath a canopy. The legend refers to the king's counting house. Another new type depicts the monarch as a Roman emperor. These new types are on larger flans than any from previous reigns.

Richard II's reign (1377-1399) was that of the last Plantagent king. The favoured emblems of this royal house - stars, crescents and fleurs-de-lys - appear regularly on jettons of the period, as do lions in reference to Crusader campaigns; but it is also in this reign that increasing numbers of Continental jettons begin to find their way to England, eventually bringing English manufacture to an end. The first flood came from Tournai (now in Belgium), but French jettons superseded them in the late-15th century. Commonest designs seem to be variations on French coats-of-arms.

It is around this time that jettons made and sold as sets for board games, rather than accounting purposes, make their appearance. Rare silver, even gold sets are known. A few jettons made by (or for) the great Italian banking houses of the period turn up in England. They were among the first to show monograms of merchants, rather than regal emblems.

The 16th century witnessed a vast flood of jettons from Nuremburg in Germany; so many that considerably more than half of all jettons found today by excavators and fieldwalkers in Britain come from that source. How and why did a relatively small German city come to dominate European jetton production for more than a century? The answer lies in social structure and the power of Nuremburg's trade guilds. The place operated as a locked-up city, by which I mean one where all apprentices became bound by strict law to a pledge that they would not leave Nuremburg once their long apprenticeship came to an end. They also intermarried and brought up their sons and daughters to follow or support the family's trade. These measures ensured that none of Nuremburg's mystery secrets and skills fell into competitors' hands. Nevertheless, they began as copyists, reproducing many French designs and undercutting the prices charged by other German cities in their ruthless campaign to dominate the business. Early output consisted of the French copies already mentioned, then a flood of small but extremely well-made jettons depicting animals, ecclesiastical figures, heraldic devices, and the famous golden apple or orb seen on numerous Nuremburg products. Few of the earliest jettons carry makers' names, but from about 1550 the practice became common. The range of designs now included pieces showing merchants at work with jettons, ships ladened with export goods, emblems of great commercial cities such as Venice – all clear indications of the beginnings of European capitalism, and of the fact that Nuremburg now dominated the jetton industry.

Identifying the names on jettons can help in dating them.
Those most likely to occur are:-

George Schultes - 1515-1559
Hans Schultes 1 - 1553-1584
Hans Schultes 2 - 1586-1603
Hans Schultes 3 - 1608-1612
Damianus Krauwinckel - 1543-1581
Egidius Krauwinckel - 1570-1613
Hans Krauwinckel 1 - 1562-1586
Hans Krauwinckel 2 - 1586-1635
Killianus Koch - 1580-?
Wolf Lauffer 1 - 1554-1601
Hans Lauffer 1 - 1584-1632
Matheus Lauffer - 1612-1634
Wolf Lauffer 2 - 1612-1631
Conrad Lauffer - 1637-1668
Wolf Lauffer 3 - 1650-1670
Lazarus Gottleib Lauffer - 1663-1709

Medieval German Jettons

Obverse and reverse of German jetton of Hanns (also Hans) Krauwinckel (circa 1580-1610).

German jetton of Hanns Krauwinckel (circa 1580-1610).

German jetton of Hanns Krauwinckel (circa 1580-1610).

German jetton of Hanns Krauwinckel (circa 1580-1610).

German jetton with obverse design of a Turk's head. The reverse shows an orb surmounted by a cross within a double tressure of three arches and three angles.

Typical Nuremburg work from the early 1600s. Hans Krauwinckel I put his name on the jetton on the right.

More from Nuremburg. The motto Das wort gotes blibt ewicke = God's Word remains eternal, is seen on the right.

The medieval jetton makers of Nuremburg turned to gaming counters in later centuries. The monarchs of Europe often featured on their work. George III was a popular portrait on counters sold in England; but this lovely example depicts Queen Anne. It may have been sold in Scotland where Anne was popular. (Photo courtesy www.agcoins.com)

Medieval German Jettons

CM

Obverse and reverse of German jetton of Hanns (also Hans) Krauwinckel (circa 1580-1610).

CM

German jetton of Hanns Krauwinckel (circa 1580-1610).

CM

German jetton of Hanns Krauwinckel (circa 1580-1610).

CM

German jetton with obverse design of a Turk's head. The reverse shows an orb surmounted by a cross within a double tressure of three arches and three angles.

CM

German jetton of Hanns Krauwinckel (circa 1580-1610).

Towards the end of the 16th century mythical and biblical scenes began to appear more frequently than the emblems of commerce, perhaps an indication that the use of reckoning counters in financial houses was drawing to a close. A further development witnessed the introduction of proverbs and trite religious messages, more interesting for their preservation of older German spellings than their morality. To provide room for longer messages and more intricate designs Nuremburg jettons became larger. Another space-saving development saw the reduction of makers' names to mere initials, but full names reappeared later, probably because rivals might have been tempted to copy initials.

In the 17th century Nuremburg turned more to making card counters and toy issues. Commoner types depict European monarchs from many reigns. Portraits of British kings and queens from Charles II to George III have come to light, some of them made from silver. The city kept up a trickle of production for other markets well into the 20th century, by which time the days of the counting board had long departed.

Among the many Old German mottos that appear on jettons, look out for:-

Anfang bedenck das endt (When beginning think of the ending)

Das wort gotes blibt ewick (God's word remains eternal)

Fleisige rechnumg macht richtikeit (Diligent accounting makes for correctness)

Getrivw handt kombt durch alle (Truth succeeds over all)

Glvck beschert ist vngewert (Fortune given is not guaranteed)

Glvck kvmbt von got alien (Luck comes from God alone)

Glvck und glas wie bald brict das (Luck and glass soon break)

Gotes segen macht reich (God's blessing brings riches)

Gott allein die eere sei (To God alone the glory)

Lib mich als ich dih (Love me as I love you)

Neydt thut ihm selbst leydt (Envy harms the envious)

Identifying Finds In The Field

Close examination of all hammered coinage finds from the 13th and 14th centuries will soon familiarise you with what to look for when identifying jettons of Edward I's reign. Anticipate these and later brass jettons on all sites, though they lie thickest in the ground on ecclesiastical sites, in city centre excavations, and on the foreshores of the River Thames.

Recommended Further Reading

Medieval English Jettons by Berry G., Spink, 1974.

Jettons, Medallets & Tokens Vol 1 by Mitchener M., Seaby, 1988.

Medieval French Jettons

French jetton from the late 16th century. Obverse shows large open jewelled crown with the wording "Ave Maria Graspinaplena". The reverse design is of an open cross terminating in fleur-de-lys with a fleur-de-lys in the centre, with the inscription "Ave Maria".

French jetton similar in design although this example has an obverse with a bust similar to that of a Roman emperor.

Nuremburg jettons 15th-18th century, as shown in an 18th century pamphlet.

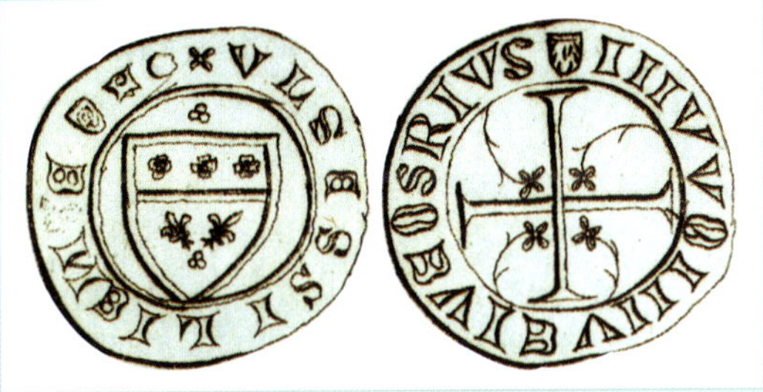

Not to scale

Chapter 4

Medieval Tokens

In the previous chapter I covered the token coinage known to have circulated as money and at certain fractional values in relation to coins of the realm. Here I turn to objects on which history remains almost silent about monetary status or value. All I can state with certainty is that tin and pewter tokens begin to turn up as finds in Britain on sites where early 13th century coin and artefact discoveries suggest economic activity, perhaps as marketplaces, or riverside wharves, or locations where people met and congregated in those days.

The tokens have a coin-like shape and size (although a little thicker), and usually have obverse/reverse designs resulting from casting in two-part moulds. The figures and emblems on many indicate strong ecclesiastical influence: mitred bishops, crosses, crosiers, pilgrims; all generally boldly executed, though primitive to modern eyes. On some the decoration has a surrounding beaded border, lending an overall impression that - whoever designed most of these tokens - had the contemporary silver coinage in mind as a model.

These early tokens have come from locations in England, Scotland and Ireland, with many discovered on medieval Church land. The use of pewter in their manufacture provides another link with religion because the ecclesiastical authorities had a monopolistic grip on pewter production in those days. The images of pilgrims strongly suggest use of tokens during pilgrimages. They may have been exchangeable for food and accommodation at certain places along pilgrimage routes; or used to pay ferrymen where the routes crossed rivers. Written evidence, mainly from France, also indicates the use of tokens as attendance tickets handed out to priests who celebrated mass at certain times of the day. But we have no information on how such tokens were later exchanged for payment or goods.

Three terms that often crop up in reference to early tokens merit mention here: Winetavern tokens; London Wall tokens; and Boy Bishop tokens. The first and second refer not to places where tokens were used, but to hoard spots – Winetavern Street in Dublin where more than 2,000 early pictorial pewter tokens were discovered in the 19th century, and London Wall, where another large hoard came to light in the 20th century.

The cult of the Boy Bishop had enthusiastic adherents throughout Europe in medieval times when many abbeys and larger churches elected a choirboy to act as the Boy Bishop during Christmastime. He dressed as a real bishop, preached sermons and handed out lead tokens to his congregations. In Britain this practice was confined mainly to East Anglia. Bury St Edmunds was the main centre, but tokens from Ely, Sudbury and Ipswich have come to light. Bury's earliest found examples date from about 1480, but the ceremony probably goes back even further, with earlier tokens yet to come to light. Recipients could use them as alms to buy food and drink at local shops. The shopkeeper would have received reimbursement from the abbey. Boy Bishop tokens have been found on East Anglian medieval market sites, evidence of their probable use as small change. This is hardly surprising as their designs imitated pennies, half groats and groats, with an obverse usually depicting St Nicholas or a bishop's mitre.

In the Guildhall Library, London there is a pamphlet titled *Two Sermons Preached By The Boy Bishop At St Paul's* and reprinted for the Camden Society in 1875. The Introduction, by Edward Rimbault, discusses "the question of money and Saint Nicholas Pence, struck for the Boy Bishop." He goes on to report that "In the Church of Saint Mary, Bury St Edmunds, in 1842, during the removal of priests' stalls, a large number of leaden pieces in imitation of

This fascinating collection of medieval lead tokens represents several years of enthusiastic fieldwalking by one Nottinghamshire enthusiast. His finds suggest that while there was regional variation in token designs outside of London, provincial developments mirrored those in the capital. Note especially the cross-and-pellet types, the pictorial anchors, sacks, animals, the initial letters and lifelike portraits and the last in the group with its triple (husband-and wife) initials and heraldic design.

Not to scale

Medieval Lead Tokens

Not to scale

Medieval Lead Tokens

Not to scale

Medieval Lead Tokens

Not to scale

Medieval & Tudor Lead Tokens

Not to scale

money were discovered. There were a dozen varieties, some the size of groats, others of pennies, thought to be imitations of coins of Edward the Sixth and his predecessors. It was possibly the practice to sink a new die each year for this coinage, which would account for the variety of types found. And it may be from design rather than accident that some were thrown behind the stalls of the church."

Presumably Rimbault means by this that unused tokens from the previous year were discarded. If he was right, the present incumbent of St Mary's should make a thorough search!

Incidentally, Rimbault is mistaken when he refers to "sinking a new die each year". These lead tokens were cast in stone moulds, one of which may be seen at Moyse's Hall Museum in Bury St Edmunds.

Returning to 13th century tokens, finds indicate a gradual transition from pewter to lead as the preferred moulding metal while the century wore on. The reason must have linked to economic hardships because although lead is cheaper, it neither looks nor wears as well as pewter; nor can mould workers cast it so thinly without risk of flaws. Lead tokens may have been made by plumbers in cities and towns, in competition with the clergy, and selling their output to merchants for secular uses. The designs on tokens also changed gradually, though with much overlapping. However, beaded borders disappeared quite early, and there was a steady reduction in diameters throughout the 13th century.

Pictorial designs showing humans gave way to shields, animals, birds and flowers, with a gradual evolution towards geometric wheel and flower designs in the early 14th century. The late 14th century witnessed a marked reduction in token sizes, as well as a thickening of flans and a growing number of lead tokens with raised edges.

In the 15th century a pronounced movement towards cross-and-pellet designs on one side of the token, often with a Gothic letter on the other side, took place.

This was followed in early Tudor times by a return to the largest size of tokens popular more than 200 years earlier. Not surprisingly, the Tudor rose and other Tudor emblems featured on many tokens at this time.

One reason why knowledge of token types and usage concentrates on medieval urban life is that massive redevelopment of London's Docklands in the 1980s presented archaeologists and mudlarks with numerous opportunities to recover medieval tokens and to suggest approximate dates for certain types by reference to hammered silver coins found nearby. Deep excavations along the banks of the Thames exposed stratified layers where pottery and

Photo courtesy Moyse's Hall Museum.

Boy Bishop token mould.

other finds also aided the dating of tokens. Most of the research results are summarized in the *British Numismatic Journal* issues referred to below as recommended further reading. The value of that research cannot be over-emphasized; but keep in mind that many tokens also come to light in the countryside.

There are references to medieval country folk calling pewter tokens "abbot's money"; this may indicate that labourers on ecclesiastical estates were paid in tokens, and that the tokens circulated locally as money. Use of pewter and/or lead discs as tallies to record work done, or crops picked, must also have occurred. Similarly, we cannot rule out the possibility that some tokens served as gaming pieces or perhaps as children's playthings.

The most probable explanation is that pewter and lead tokens of the 13th, 14th and 15th centuries were ecclesiastical money, pilgrims' tickets, fractions of sterling pennies in busy marketplaces, tallies for crop pickers and other casual workers, gaming counters for adults and playthings for children – serving all of these purposes in a rich overlapping of human activities.

Coming now to the reign of Elizabeth I, I can usefully begin with a quote from a book titled **A View Of The Copper Coinage Of England, Including The Late Tin And Latten Tokens Made By Tradesmen During the Reign Of Elizabeth** written by Thomas Snelling in 1770. Complaining about the lack of silver farthings, he wrote: "In all well regulated governments it is owned to be requisite that there should be money of small value for the use of the market and the poorer sort of subjects, as of the larger pieces for other purposes of trade and commutation. And what the value of the smallest pieces should be is pointed out by the proportion the price of provisions bear to that of labour and the ability of the lower class of people to purchase them. A farthing, or the fourth part of a penny, and its double, the halfpenny, are those of the least value we have ever had in England, and began to be coined about the year 1270 under Edward the First of silver stan-

Boy Bishop Tokens

These are mainly from Bury St Edmunds with a few from Ely.
Please note the last two pieces are tentatively allocated.

CM

CM

CM

CM

CM

CM

CM

CM

Boy Bishop Tokens

Boy Bishop token?

Boy Bishop token?

Obverse and reverse of 16th century lead Boy Bishop token; mitre on obverse, reverse cross and pellets, Bury St Edmunds type.

Obverse and reverse of unofficial token of the reign of Elizabeth I, circa 1574. Fleurs between two pillars obverse, reverse rampant lion crown with legend.

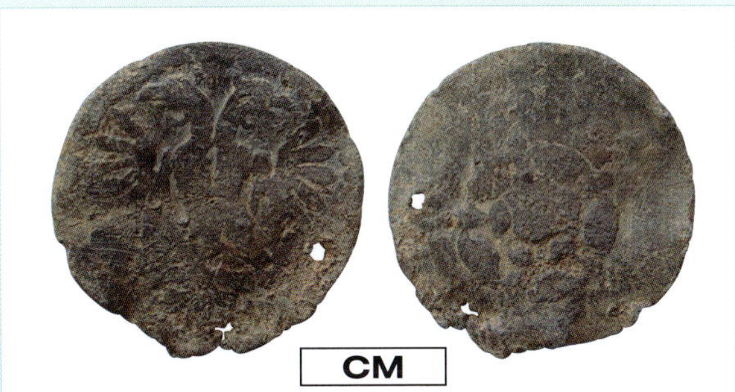

Obverse and reverse of unofficial token circa 1574. Obverse double-headed eagle, reverse Tudor rose with legend "God Save The Quene".

Obverse and reverse of unofficial token circa 1574. Obverse three fleurs de lys within shield, crown above pillar to each side. Reverse lion rampant with legend.

Obverse and reverse of Elizabeth I unofficial lead token dating 1574. Double headed eagle obverse.

Obverse and reverse of Boy Bishop penny token, Bury St Edmunds type, 16th century. "Sanctvs Nicholavs" on obverse.

Obverse and reverse of Boy Bishop penny token, small mitre, Bury St Edmunds type, 16th century.

dard .... [Owing to gradual reductions in weight] ... the farthing could be minted no longer of good silver, being lost almost as fast as coined, no other method remained of striking them but of base silver or pure copper. And the legislature not taking either method, and they being much wanted for many purposes, shopkeepers and tradesmen made tokens of themselves."

On evidence of finds dated to Elizabeth's reign, what many of them made (or had made) were crudely cast and rather thick lead discs, almost all bearing one or two initial letters in Roman style. Genealogical research in some districts has confirmed the initials belonged to landowners. We cannot tell whether those finds are tallies or local token coinage, but it is worth noting that large numbers of casual labourers who often worked for less than one penny a day needed payment for their efforts at picking, harvesting and carrying farm produce, or hauling boats along rivers, or dragging carts out of mud, and many similarly menial yet essential tasks. A local token currency in fractions of a penny, however much frowned upon by higher authorities, would have suited local needs admirably.

Snelling also refers to proposals made to Queen Elizabeth for the production of "farthing pledges and halfpenny pledges" in copper, and for these new pledges "to be made current in all the Queen's dominions, so that every person was obliged to receive them for all payments below twenty shillings." As usual, the monarch declined to go ahead with the scheme, but the author reports that he saw patterns of these pledges, and that they had an ER monogram and crown on one side, and a rose crown on the other surrounded by the words "The Pledge Of A Halfpenny". He also saw a similar pattern penny pledge dated 1601. He goes on to mention Bristol's official square-shaped copper farthings of 1577, sanctioned by Elizabeth for circulation in and up to 10 miles around Bristol. Of even greater interest to us here, he adds that before that date Bristol, Worcester and Oxford struck city farthings in lead and "latten"; while in London "no less than three thousand people made their own lead tokens." Bristol's first design depicted "a coney" (rabbit), while Worcester's had "a death's head". He also illustrates a London lead token dated 1599. Its obverse and reverse carry the initial R.C. and show a cow (?) about to be slaughtered. He describes its general shape as "having more the appearance of a dump than of money." and he writes that such lead pieces "could be found in any tavern or chandler's shop."

Towards the end of Elizabeth's reign advertising occurs on tokens, usually in the form of a pictorial emblem that must surely have been an inn sign - cock, bull, eagle, etc. The arms of a few city guilds (bakers, tailors, etc.) also make their appearance for the first time, but by no means the last, as I shall demonstrate in later chapters. However, the dominant type remained a dumpy lead piece bearing initials on one or both sides.

Space permitting, I hope to illustrate within this chapter a most interesting collection of 89 lead tokens found over many years by a fieldwalking enthusiast in Nottinghamshire. All were recovered from open fields within definite parish boundaries. Such finds, when they carry initials, provide opportunities for further research in parish records. In many cases we can name the token's issuer, locate his address, read about his occupation, his neighbours and more. I hope fieldwalkers in other counties will form similar collections and compare them with the Nottinghamshire finds.

Identifying Finds In The Field

Lead does not survive well in plough soil rich in organic matter. Expect finds from such sites to have thick coatings of corrosion. Those of modern 1p–10p size need careful examination for signs of moulded lettering or designs. Pewter or tin will be thinner and darker, often showing fewer signs of corrosion. On wet sites lead survives remarkably well. It also stands up well to burial in clay. Take careful note of dated or dateable adjacent finds such as coins and pottery fragments. If you have initials to work with check parish records via the Genuki website.

Recommended Further Reading

English Tokens, c.1200 AD to 1425 AD by Mitchiner M. and Skinner A., British Numismatic Journal, 1983.
English Tokens, c. 1425 to 1672 by Mitchiner M. and Skinner A., British Numismatic Journal, 1984.

Chapter 5

17th Century Tokens

Let me begin with a typical outburst from a fiery Elizabeth I in 1576: "*We observe a long continued and yet very intolerable and arrogant disorder used by private persons in making tokens of lead and tin, and generally coined and put out instead of our small monies by grocers, vintners, chandlers, alehouse keepers, and diverse other persons.*"

Her complaint that the new three-halfpenny and three-farthing pieces she had ordered to be minted in 1561 had not stopped the fashioning of crude moulds, and the flow of molten lead into them, in every county in England and Wales seems fully justified when we glance at the issues covered in a previous chapter. Yet Elizabeth and all earlier monarchs had only themselves to blame for their failures to grasp the nettle of token coinage with a face value greater than its intrinsic value, and backed by a regal guarantee of its face worth. Turn to your Seaby's **Coins of England** and look at the illustration showing a halfpenny of 1582. Try to put yourself in the worn boots of an Elizabethan farm labourer in Leicestershire earning a penny a day. Would you have felt financially secure carrying your day's earnings as two tiny coins such as those? Far safer and more satisfying to feel the weight of four leaden farthings in your back pocket as you plodded your weary way homeward. And my question makes the optimistic assumption that enough of the new silver coins would circulate as far as 100 miles beyond the capital when workers at the Mint spent so much of their time complaining that there was little or no profit in making this small money due to rising silver prices.

The above paragraph sets the scene for what was to become a cascade of token copper and brass in the next century, but Elizabeth had one more diatribe against private token makers when she took the mayor of Bristol to task in 1577 for tolerating "*persons in Bristol without any manner of authority to frame and stamp in lead and brass certain farthing tokens of sundry sorts and making, uttering them to their private uses in exchange for money in several trades and occupations.*" The mayor defended the practice on the grounds that Bristol's merchants needed large numbers of farthings to settle daily payments to cargo handlers in the city's busy docks. This special plea resulted in Royal sanction for an issue of square Bristol token farthings in brass. Some 28,000 pieces were struck and distributed in the following year; not enough to meet the demands of all who clamoured after these useful pieces of money. Within another year more than 100,000 were produced and some of them reached London. Struck on a 20mm square flan with the letters "CB" (for Civitas Bristol) on the obverse and the arms of the city (a ship setting sail from a castle) on the reverse, several issues of this token served Bristol's small change needs for the next six years.

The succeeding monarch, James I, (1603-1625) had already issued copper money; indeed his forebears had lived with coppers in Scotland for several centuries, and the Scottish denomination known as "turners" had circulated in northern England as token farthings long before James came to the English throne. After a decade of running his expensive English court, shortage of funds encouraged the king to stoop to farthing production in 1613; but he astutely avoided soiling his own hands with English coppers by granting a licence to his friend Lord Harrington on the understanding that if the monarch put up the bulk of the money required to buy the copper, then the bulk of the profits must come to the Crown. An investment of £24,000 on metal brought a profit of £65,000. Lord Harrington received £25,000; the monarch took the remaining £40,000.

The examples here, randomly picked from tens of thousands of private farthings, halfpennies and pennies issued between 1640 and 1670, illustrate the rich variety of imagery, lettering, designs, dates, self-promotion and history recorded on these fascinating finds.

Not to scale

Privately Issued Tokens 1640-1670

Not to scale

Obverse and reverse of a Kings Lyn (Lynne) farthing dated 1669.

Obverse and reverse of Diss farthing, 1669. Reverse anchor above shield.

Obverse and reverse of farthing of Peter Barker of Norfolk, dated 1656.

Obverse and reverse of token farthing dated 1660, issued by Francis Arwak(e/er), of Chelmsford.

Obverse and reverse of halfpenny token of Gt Yarmouth Borough showing arms of same, 1669.

Obverse and reverse of farthing token of John Freebourne of Witham, clothier, dated 1667.

Obverse and reverse of Charles I Harrington copper farthing, issued under Royal licence.

Obverse and reverse of rare small Harrington farthing, tinned copper to give the appearance of hammered coin. Issued in reign of James I under royal licence.

Obverse and reverse of farthing token, Bishops Stortford, Edward Aynsworth, circa mid 1660s reverse reindeer with wording "Ye Raine Deare".

Obverse and reverse of farthing token of Christopher Hey, Mercer of Watton, circa mid 1660s.

Obverse and reverse of farthing of Thomas Hudson of Woolpit dated 1664.

Obverse and reverse of rose farthing of Charles I, issued under royal licence.

Obverse and reverse of halfpenny token of John Gray wine copper White Cross Street, Middlesex, circa mid 1660s.

Obverse and reverse of halfpenny token of Mary Curtis of Chelmsford, dated 1667.

Obverse and reverse of "A Farthing For Axmister".

The chequerboard image on this piece may have been an inn sign. Board games were very popular in taverns of this age.

The first Harrington issues were on small flans with a surface coating of tin, possibly to continue the fiction of a silver coinage. In 1634 Lord Maltravers purchased the licence; but due to widespread forgery the design changed to include a small brass plug, which made forgery very difficult. Similar patents granted in the reign of Charles I (1625-1649) were used to defraud merchants and shopkeepers who paid too much for the copper content, then suffered greater loss when the patentees refused to change their farthings for silver, claiming that all returned farthings were forgeries. Public outrage caused Parliament to suppress the issue in 1644 and make plans for an alternative official farthing. But the execution of the king in 1649 removed the exclusive royal prerogative of coining money. Desperate for small change, tradesmen began almost at once to issue their own.

Londoners had easy access to the skills of die-cutters who worked at the Tower Mint, and it seems highly likely that men from that establishment cut the dies and coined the farthings for the several London tavern-keepers who rushed into issuing their own change within a few months of the king's death. More than 3,000 enterprising London individuals (publicans, grocers, mercers, butchers, chandlers, fishmongers, coffee-house keepers, bakers, fruiterers, shoemakers, tobacconists, and several dozen other trades) joined in during the next few years. Within a decade the use-your-own-brass-farthings policy had swept across the country from Northumberland to Cornwall. Wales joined in by 1664; Ireland not long after. Only Scotland, where nobody suffered from a shortage of official coppers, declined to take part. Nevertheless, it seems probable that up to 20,000 issuers did their bit to relieve the 17th century small change famine.

A typical private farthing of the period measured slightly less than our decimal 1p, struck in copper or brass on a circular flan. The issuer's name was prominent on the obverse; if not, then his initials probably occupied a central position, with part of his address.... also boldly announced. In London that might be a street name, or parish, or prominent landmark; in the provinces a village might be mentioned. Reverses commonly displayed the arms of the man's trade guild, or a symbol to typify his business. Space permitting, the issue year might also appear on the token. On a large number of specimens three initials in a triangular formation occur, signifying a man-and-wife enterprise; the surname initial always above, the husband's to left and the wife's to right. Legends often flowed from obverse to reverse. The central part, or field, is usually separated from the outer by a dotted line, or cable-patterned border. From the early 1660s there was more use of script lettering instead of capitals, and one or both sides filled entirely with a legend.

That brief description shows why token finds from this period always delight fieldwalkers and archaeologists. To obtain such a wealth of information on so small an artefact is a rare pleasure, and extremely helpful to genealogists and local historians. More tantalising is the very strong possibility that hundreds, perhaps thousands of hitherto unrecorded token farthings await discovery a few inches beneath the soil, or in forgotten boxes and drawers in old houses and business premises.

The men from the Mint (if indeed they made the dies) rarely signed their work. Only David Ramage, an official engraver at the Tower Mint, marked his dies with the letter "R". Characteristics of his workmanship, including a five-star mullet mark (a cross with straight-edged rays) and lozenge-shaped stops between words/letters, together with his mark, appear on a widely dispersed group of tokens. This suggests that London token makers may have supplied provincial issuers. A general uniformity of design features on very many tokens supports this view. It has also been suggested by some authorities that the business relied on travelling salesmen who took examples of tokens made for London issuers on journeys around the country when securing orders. The new dies were probably sold to issuers so that they could carry out further stampings locally.

Halfpenny and a very few penny tokens appeared in the 1660s, the halfpence often not much larger than an average farthing; the penny up to the size of a modern 2p. Even more uncommon are tokens struck on square, diamond, octagonal and heart-shaped flans. Extra areas of metal available on these shapes usually allowed an issuer to provide additional information about his business. In other words, odd shapes were probably introduced to catch the public's eye and advertise one's wares. The first appearance of token halfpennies coincides with the withdrawal of Commonwealth silver coins in 1661; the restored monarchy of Charles II (1660-1685) omitted halfpence from the new silver coinage, thereby perpetuating the need for tokens. Demand for pennies may have had links with the growth in popularity of London coffee houses where that was the price of a cup of the new beverage.

Many local authorities looked with envy on tradesmen's tokens and quickly realised the benefits of having municipal small change, especially when it came to paying tiny amounts of money to "deserving" poor folk who crammed town and city workhouses to do jobs such as oakum picking or wash-house scrubbing for the price of soup and bread. Bristol, where the first city tokens had arrived in Queen Elizabeth's reign, issued its first 17th century token farthing in 1652. A hundred other towns and cities followed, though surprisingly London did not join in. Phrases such as *For The Relief Of The Poor and Payable At The Workhouse*, or mention of officials such as beadles, mayors, churchwardens and

Examples of Trade Guild emblems.

These often appeared on the reverses of 17th century tokens.

Cordwainers

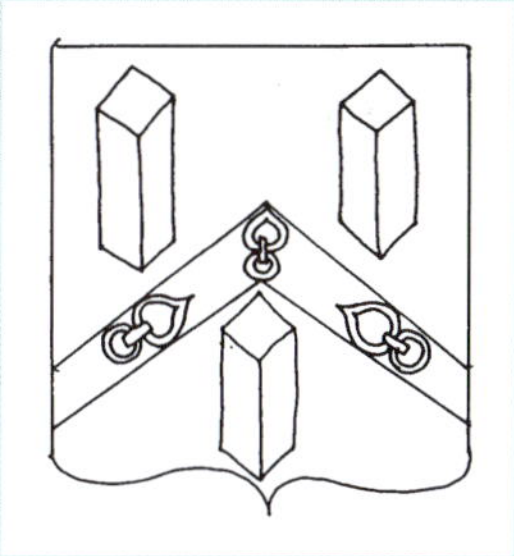

Ironmongers

Mercers

Watermen

Drapers

Fishmongers

Stationers

Innkeepers

Butchers

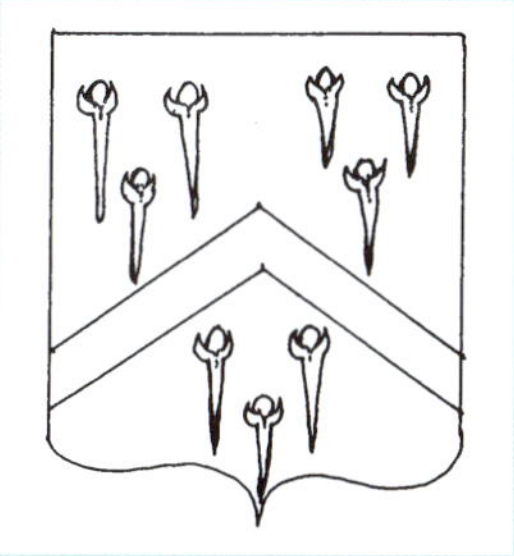

Grocers

Bakers

Apothecaries

Not to scale

Bristol was the only city to issue brass tokens in the reign of Elizabeth I. When the 17th century wave of token production began Bristol again led the field with this lovely example based on the original design, the main difference being that 16th century issues were struck on square flans.

overseers readily identify these issues. They were struck in much greater quantities than private traders' money; thus they occur more frequently as finds.

This prolific period of copper token issues stuttered to a close when Charles II finally agreed to mint regal coppers. His proclamation of 1672 reads: *"Our subjects would not easily be wrought upon to accept the farthings and half-pence of these private stampers if there were not some kind of necessity for small coins for public use, which cannot well be done in silver, nor safely in any other metal, unless the intrinsic value of the coin be equal, or near to that value for which it is made current ... [The Mint will] ... make half-pence and farthings to contain as much copper in weight as shall be of the true intrinsic value ... after charges of coining and uttering are deducted."*

Fine words; but only 40,000 of the new coppers were minted up to 1676. Counterfeiting with lower weights had become widespread by the end of the century. A new wave of tokens was bound to follow in the next century.

Identifying Finds In The Field

The description of a typical 17th century copper token given above will greatly assist initial identification. Further investigation to track the issuer, if unknown, requires searches in local archives. This aspect of token collecting has become much easier in recent years thanks to the availability on the Internet of the Genuki pages provided by groups of dedicated genealogists, many of them ardent token collectors.

The vast majority of 17th century tokens offered for sale are in F-grade or poorer, and almost certainly came to light as a result of fieldwalking or archaeological excavation. Finds from the Thames foreshores and from clay ground often display attractive dark patina; but finds from acidic soils inevitably suffer corrosion, especially so when the tokens were struck on thin flans. Patient work with a magnifying glass may be necessary to elucidate all information available on the token's surface.

Recommended Further Reading

British Tokens And Their Values by Seaby P., Seaby Publications, 1974.
Seventeenth Century England: Traders & Their Tokens by Berry G., Seaby Publications, 1988.

Chapter 6

18th Century Tokens

Evasions, Commercial Tokens, Advertising Tokens, Collectors' Tokens, General Circulation Tokens, Spurious Tokens & Downright Forgeries.

"Awash with false and featureless money" is how one Londoner described the capital at the start of George III's reign in 1760. "And of good money, none to be had."

Little wonder, with the Royal Mint's antiquated machinery falling apart and barely meeting demand for gold and silver issues, that so many forgers got their livings from false coppers. Sixteen years passed between 1754, the last year of issue of regal small change in the reign of George II and the first George III coppers of 1770, which meant that few children in the country had ever seen a legally newly-minted penny, halfpenny or farthing.

Forty years earlier George I had issued a few dumpy copper halfpennies and farthings between 1717 and 1724; Queen Anne did likewise for one year, 1714. That's why "featureless" coppers of William III and even tin farthings of James II, all worn quite smooth from passing hand-to-hand for almost a century, rattled in the tills of distraught shopkeepers and tavern owners in Georgian London and throughout the provinces.

Counterfeiting was treason, a hanging offence; though some readers might agree that matters had improved a little since the days of Henry I, who, in 1124, ordered severing of the right hand and testicles of those who meddled with his coinage. One way in which 18th century counterfeiters dodged the consequences of capture was to make their forgeries sufficiently different from coins of the realm that they could claim to be copying foreign tokens, which was not a crime in England. For example, a 1699 farthing of William III had an obverse legend that reads: *Gulielmus Tertius* and a reverse with the word *Britannia*.

Crafty counterfeiters, relying rather heavily on the limited reading abilities of farthing users, made fakes good enough to pass as worn money, but with legends such as *Gulielmus Shakespear ... Englands Glory*. Other popular phrases included *Pitt Rex* on a coin with the monarch's bust so worn it might have been anyone; *Bonny Girl*, on another reverse depicting Britannia; and *Prince of the Isles* on an Irish halfpenny.

Counterfeiters sold them at half face value to wholesalers who resold them at 30 shillings face value for one gold guinea. By the middle of the century half of all coppers in circulation were counterfeit; by 1787 a Royal Mint official declared that "only eight percent of all copper coins in circulation bear some tolerable resemblance to the King's coin." These forged oddities, known collectively as "evasions", form a popular branch of token collecting today.

The machinery and tools used in the 18th century factories, mines and workshops provide industrial archaeologists with useful information on technology and factory conditions of the times. Included below are some examples.

Household products on 18th century tokens - boot blacking.

Social history on 18th century tokens. A fine view of Lowestoft in 1795 showing bathing machines on the beach.

Social conditions referred to on 18th century tokens - debtors' prison.

Advertising on 18th century tokens. Here's one offering "Fine Teas Of The Rough Flavour"!

The "Pro Bono Publico" on this example means "For The Public Good" although it carries no information on how or where to redeem it.

Not to scale

Tokens promoting industry and manufacture

Not to scale

18th century Donald & Co token. Obverse provides a firm promise to pay. Reverse providing an accurate address for repayments.

Obverse & Reverse of John Wilkinson token. This Iron Master was lampooned in the press for posing like George III on his tokens.

Obverse & reverse of 18th century Manchester halfpenny. The problem with these general issue tokens was that they failed to tell customers where they could be redeemed.

Obverse & reverse of token of military or patriotic theme extolling the "Wooden Walls Of Old England".

Not to scale

Obverse & reverse of token of the military or patriotic group of "Pro Rege" type.

The face that launched a collecting mania. The druid on the first token issued by the Parys Mine Company. Thousands of manufacturers, merchants and shopkeepers followed this lead.

Obverse of Conder token. James Conder, liner draper, later became the author of the standard reference work on 18th century tokens.

Not to scale

Obverse and reverse of Thomas Hardy halfpenny token, dated 1794, tried for high treason and acquitted.

Obverse and reverse of token halfpenny "Ships, colonies, & commerce". Reverse sailing ship. Circa 1790s.

Obverse and reverse of M. Banbury token "Rusher, Hatter, Bookseller & Stationer".

Obverse and reverse of halfpenny token commemorating Dr. Samuel Johnson.

Not to scale

Passing a dodgy halfpenny in a crowded Fleet Street alehouse carried few risks; but consider the problems of manufacturers in the busy towns of the Midlands and the north, where pay packets came under scrutiny from disgruntled employees every week. Sharp eyes would have spotted a counterfeit at once and perhaps organised a riot. What could the ironmasters, mine sinkers and mill owners do when faced with such urgent necessity? One solution lay in asking half-a-dozen workmen to share a single pound note. (Paper money had been introduced to alleviate the problems of guinea shortages). The workmen, or their wives, had to put up with the inconvenience of shopping as a group until they collected enough change to work out who owed what to whom, and probably to squabble over who had to accept the forgeries that had somehow crept in. And the more the wheels of industry gathered pace, the greater the need for small change.

Fittingly the man who came up with the solution owned his own copper mine on the Isle of Anglesey; the very mine from which Romans had extracted copper to make barbarous radiates and minims 1400 years earlier. The location of the rich seam had remained lost throughout recorded history until a man fossicking for ores stumbled upon it just seven feet beneath the surface. The mine's owner was Thomas Williams, an industrialist soon to earn the sobriquet "Copper King Williams". He employed more than 1,000 men whose job was to blow up Parys Mountain, dig out the rich ore, and transport it to the company's smelters.

Exasperated at not finding enough pence to fill his men's pay packets, he took a consignment of ore to a smelting works in Holywell, set up a minting machine and made token coins exactly one-ounce in weight, the value of one penny's worth of copper at that time (1787). It proved a momentous year in the story of tokens, though initially Williams had no other thought than to pay his workmen. To declare to the Crown that he was not forging coin of the realm, he put a cowled figure of an ancient druid on the obverse of his tokens, and the initials of his business, Parys Mine Company, on the reverse, together with the crucial words "We Promise To Pay The Bearer One Penny".

You may have come across an example because Williams went on to coin 250 tons of pennies and 50 tons of halfpennies during subsequent years. Production was shortly moved to Birmingham where local shopkeepers, weary of worn money and impressed by the true weight and boldness of striking, snapped up the Parys Mine Company tokens and treated them as sound currency.

Wherever workers stood in line for their pay packets during the next few years they could rely on receiving coppers of good weight because their employer copied the Welsh innovation and either made the company's own tokens, or sent off orders to token makers who sprang up in Birmingham and London to satisfy demand. Many of the tokens depicted machinery and equipment used by the men and women whose labours produced the profits. That must have made them even more acceptable to the workforce; it certainly increases interest in collecting them nowadays, especially the interest of industrial archaeologists who can examine on the surfaces of these pictorial pieces extraordinarily good illustrations of forges, iron ships, canal locks, and the tools of numerous long-lost manufacturing processes. Before long, any shopkeeper or small merchant prepared to invest a few tens of pounds could order sufficient tokens to meet his local need for change.

In the 17th century farthings had fulfilled the requirements of the average shopkeeper; in the 18th century halfpennies were preferred. So long as shopping customers could locate his premises by information stamped on his tokens; and provided the tokens had the correct weight and carried that crucial phrase "Payable On Demand" and he demonstrated ability to do that, the tradesman could feel reasonably safe from prosecution when handing them out in change; however; it did remain the case that token issuing broke the law. Confident that a government relieved of the problem of small change would turn a blind eye, thousands of small businesses became token issuers in the 1780s-90s, with designs ever more elaborate and attractive.

Thick flans offered a tempting edge on which to impress information about where to redeem the tokens. In many cases the extra space thus available on the obverse and/or reverse provided more room for promotion; indeed advertising often became the primary reason for issuing the pieces. Some firms began to omit their promise to pay. Their tokens were plainly intended as advertising and usually gave great prominence to the name of the issuer on the obverse, while omitting any mention of value, though they still handed out their tokens as substitute halfpennies. Nevertheless, such pieces ought to be regarded as advertising tokens, despite the clear evidence from finds of worn specimens that they circulated as small change and in fairly large numbers.

A glance at the illustrations accompanying this chapter shows how very attractive these utilitarian items must have appeared to a general public long accustomed to worn money. Token makers were delighted to discover that men and women in no way connected with the businesses depicted on the pieces began to acquire them as collectors' items. And even more pleased to find customers willing to pay well above the face value of a halfpenny to obtain an attractive and uncirculated specimen. As the fad swept the nation manufacturers responded with pieces solely for collectors - architectural, scenic, historical, political figures, and especially serialised sets

18th Century Tokens of Essex

Forming a collection of 18th century tokens from one county offers fascinating challenges to the collector and amateur historian. Illustrated are a few examples from the collection of Ivan Buck.

Epping shilling.

Braintree halfpenny.

Chelmsford halfpenny.

Colchester halfpenny.

Dunmow halfpenny.

Warley halfpenny.

Maldon halfpenny.

Woodford halfpenny.

Woodford farthing. (These pieces are rare and were made from the centre of the halfpenny dies).

Leigh farthing.

that required multiple purchases. Some collectors even paid manufacturers to have small lots made as presents for friends and fellow enthusiasts of the new hobby. Many were superb miniature works of art; but because production runs were so small they never circulated as any kind of money. Today's collectors often refer to them as "private tokens".

In connection with the collecting fad I must mention James Conder, linen draper and token collecting fanatic. He had a token made for his own Tavern Street, Ipswich shop. It depicted the town's market cross on the obverse and promoted the drapery business on the reverse. Conder liked it so much he began collecting examples of other traders' tokens; at first locally; then county-wide; then nationwide; and then throughout the colonies. It led to the publication of his 1798 catalogue **An Arrangement Of Provincial Coins, Tokens & Medalettes Issued in Great Britain, Ireland, and the Colonies**. It became the token collectors' bible and it remained the standard work on the subject for more than 80 years. Even today many American and British collectors refer to their 18th century tokens as "Conders".

The demise of 18th century tokens began with issues carrying phrases such as "For General Circulation and Payable Anywhere", which, of course, meant that nobody had pledged to redeem them for coin of the realm. The weight of these pieces is often considerably less than tokens issued by specified traders and merchants; the workmanship is usually crude and probably emanated from cut-price metal bashers in down-market districts of Birmingham. That's how the profits on them were made. They sold by the score to lowly shopkeepers who could not afford to place orders themselves, but who nevertheless needed change. Some may have circulated alongside the pieces of lead covered in a previous chapter.

As token makers vied for increased sales the unscrupulous began to sell specious pieces apparently issued by firms not recorded in any trade directories; or by small businesses in remote parts of the country who found out only years later that their names had appeared on tokens. The production of mules (obverse and reverse match-ups from obsolete dies) and of deliberate errors passed off as rarities; even cheap imitations of expensive tokens sold to poorer collectors further down the social scale, became the main work of the day for many in the tokens business. Sets of these specious pieces often went to market as gaming counters, but with a nod and a wink they often passed as money in pubs, markets and other places where coins changed hands quickly.

By 1797 the amount of fraudulent tokens was so great the government was driven to action. A contract was issued for a supply of official copper "cartwheel" two-pence and pennies, to be struck at the Soho manufactory of Boulton & Watt, with halfpennies and farthings following in 1799. At the same time the issuing of tokens was declared illegal. But a new century would bring yet more tokens, and not simply mere coppers.

Identifying Finds In The Field

As with 17th century tokens, these finds invariably have sufficient information on their surfaces to satisfy finders' curiosity. Specialist collectors have no interest in worse than F grade 18th century tokens likely to be found by fieldwalkers; but if your interest lies in social history a find like this can lead to fascinating detective work when you try to track down the location of a small shop or factory. Nice specimens sometimes turn up at house clearance sales.

Recommended Further Reading

The Provincial Token Coinage of the 18th Century by R. Dalton and S.H. Hamer.
Trade Tokens. A Social and Economic History by J.R.S. Whiting, 1971
The Token Tracer. An Index of Token Legends 1700-1860 by J. Whitmore. 1990.
Commercial Coins 1787-1804 by R.C. Bell. 1963.

Chapter 7

Communion Tokens

The grip religion held on human minds in centuries past seems quite irrational to the godless majority as we walk today's city streets and observe derelict churches and abandoned churchyards on every side. Yet in early medieval times a single city parish church needed several priests to celebrate its multiple daily services and tend to the needs of its parishioners, who crammed the pews to faithfully observe the rituals of the Mass in the sure and certain knowledge that Judgement Day's dawn was almost upon them and Beelzebub would roast them in Hell for unrepented sins. Priests being human, the weaknesses of the flesh – oversleeping, indulging in too much church wine, doing the sort of things priests got up to in Chaucer's **Canterbury Tales** - tempted them as much as the congregation. Their moral frailty created a need for bishops to devise some means of recording priests' attention to their duties.

It is in those practices that the origins of communion tokens lie. There is some documentary evidence from France that stamped pieces of lead, perhaps similar to the Boy Bishop tokens already discussed, were given to priests to tally the duties they had carried out. If we bear in mind that in those days there was but a single Church for the whole of Christendom, we can safely assume that similar systems operated in England.

The transition from recording the activities of priests to checking on the congregation probably occurred at some moment of perceived moral danger when the Roman Catholic Church felt under threat from breakaway sects such as Lollards, Hussites and – most dangerous to the hierarchy – Martin Luther. In turn the leaders of these groups would have looked upon keeping watchful eyes on their Protestant members as a sacred duty.

Both the Holy Catholic and the Reformed Church in France were using communion tokens in the 1560s. Dutch Protestants followed suit in the 1580s; and in England by the time of Elizabeth I's reign tallies had evolved to the status of tickets that had to be purchased in order to gain admission to Holy Communion services. In 1592 St Saviour's Church, Southwark sold more than 2,000 such leaden tickets at two pence each; by 1620 the price had risen to three pence per token. Many other English church records refer to "Communion Halfpence", so perhaps Southwark overcharged. In the Diocese of Durham in the late 16th century the Easter Reckonings were lists of parishioners who had paid for their communion tokens, and those who had not.

Scottish Presbyterian ministers followed the instructions of John Calvin who urged the use of tokens as a means of barring unworthy persons from their services. In 17th century Scotland all Reformers suffered persecution during the reign of Catholic Stuarts. They had to hold their Communion services in secret once or twice each year, often meeting out of doors in secluded spots. To protect themselves from spying eyes they issued tokens to trusted members. Inevitably, the tokens took on the significance of holy relics. Local leaders had to be present when a trusted blacksmith melted and cast the lead or pewter from which they were made. In some cases the tokens were gathered in after the Communion and melted down to ensure that searches by Catholic authorities would fail to find incriminating evidence. Fortunately, not all ministers adopted these measures, so a few of the earliest tokens survive. Their workmanship is often crude, with no more than an initial or two on the surface, perhaps indicating a church (kirk) or a minister's name. By the time persecution ended in the 1690s with the establishment of the Church of Scotland, the use of tokens had become part of the ritual.

A fine collection of Scottish Communion tokens showing a variety of shapes and inscriptions.

A fine collection of Scottish Communion tokens showing a variety of shapes and inscriptions. Note also the incised number "2" on the Urquhart lozenge-shaped example.

CM

Descriptions of Scottish services in the early 19th century throw some light on the tokens most commonly found and collected today. All potential communicants were obliged to attend Bible classes prior to the main service. Those who successfully passed examination received a token. By that time most tokens were machine-made in pewter or lead and inscribed not only with the initials or name of the kirk, but also with a suitable religious quotation of the "Do this in remembrance of me" variety. A few tokens carried dates, and some had the name of the minister.

Of greater importance was the word "Table", after which a number would have been punched into the metal before the token was handed to the successful communicant. The number told him/her at which table to sit during the service. On the appointed day tables were placed in a clearing not far from the kirk's door and set out with communion wine and bread. Each person sat at the table allocated on the token. The number of tables required obviously depended upon the number of parishioners. One to 10 seems the average, with up to 40 people at each. However, it is recorded that in 1791 a church in Perthshire set out 29 tables to accommodate the 2,361 token holders who took part.

Presbyterian ministers seem to have purchased and retained their own tokens in those days, taking them to a different kirk if they moved to a new parish, and re-using them even if they bore the old church's name or initials. But in other branches of the faith – Episcopalians, Lutherans, Methodists, Baptists, etc – members of the congregation kept their tokens and took them home after the service. Lost tokens of that type must form the bulk of those found today.

I have already mentioned that dated tokens were uncommon. The earliest dated seem to be "Carsphaim 1648" but other dated 17th century specimens have been found. In the 18th century it became common practice to indicate the kirk's name in full. In the 19th century tokens sometimes carried suitable pictorial embellishments such as burning bushes, communion vessels, Bibles, tables, fishes, doves, lambs and crosses. The emblems of local authorities and patrons of the church also occur.

After 1850 pictorial individuality gave way to stock designs offered by commercial diesinkers. Shapes included round, square, oblong, oval, hearts and lozenges. Copper, brass, bronze, and even aluminium was used to make tokens, but lead and lead alloys remained the commonest metals until the dawn of the 20th century when most metallic tokens were superseded by printed cards.

The Scots are renowned as emigrants. They carried the token issuing habit to the United States, Canada, Australia, New Zealand and other parts of the world. Spreading token use in this way has left more than 6,000 different token types for collectors worldwide to look out for.

Identifying Finds In The Field

Any fragments of lead found close to old churches should be carefully examined; they could turn out to be early, even unrecorded tokens. Some Scottish enthusiasts obtain the bulk of their tokens by attending house clearance sales and buying unsorted button boxes where old communion tokens often end up.

Recommended Further Reading

Auld Kirk Tokens by Anderson J., 1903.
Communion Tokens Of The World by Burzinski L.M., 1999.

Chapter 8

19th Century Base Metal & Silver Tokens

The Government's solution to the late 18th century blight of underweight and unredeemable copper tokens had been to put full-weight regal pence back into circulation. This was initially, in 1797, with massive "cartwheel" penny and two-penny pieces, followed, in 1799, by large regal halfpennies and farthings. The public took to the new money at once with enthusiastic disregard for the uncomfortable drag on pocket and purse caused by a shilling's worth of two-penny pieces.

The economy may have stumbled into the 19th century encumbered by a great weight of change, but at least it seemed free of the fraudsters. On the other hand, Britain faced another 15 years of warfare to defeat Bonaparte, while many of the mills and manufactories of the Midlands and the north worked flat-out to meet demands for the weapons and accoutrements of war. Copper was in great demand. It had cost £105 per ton when the cartwheel coins were minted; by 1808 the same ton cost £200. Cartwheel coppers went into private furnaces as fast as smelters could shovel them. The Government hurriedly reduced the weight of its halfpennies and farthings in 1806/07 and refused, in the light of copper's value, to mint more. Nothing official in coppers was to come into circulation until 1821. So the scene was set for a renewed burst of token manufacture and use.

Many a battered and worn flan from the previous century had to stand-in as a countermarked token in the 19th century. Halfpennies of George II and George III, whether genuine or forgeries, received a new lease of life in this way. Even spurious 18th century tokens that people had thrown away as worthless a decade earlier, came back as countermarked pence, with another firm's name, trade and address stamped or punched over that of the previous issuer. But demand always outstripped supply. By 1811, and following another refusal by the Government to come to the aid of industry, a group of token makers in Birmingham took up the challenge and began pressing new pieces for industrial and commercial concerns throughout Britain, with greatest demand felt in those places where steam engines powered factories that needed large workforces and many small wage-packets.

Two centuries earlier private farthings had predominated; the 18th century had witnessed halfpennies as the most popular token value; but in the 19th century pennies accounted for the bulk of copper output. The model seems to have been the defunct cartwheel penny with a large flan that offered lots of scope for eye-catching designs, though most tokens of this century have utilitarian images and use a lot of the extra space for larger lettering. Promises regarding redeeming now often include phrases such as *One Pound Note Given In Exchange For 240 Tokens*.

The industrialisation of the landscape is reflected in the many views of factories, furnaces, smelting works, mine workings, smoking chimneys, forges and anvils seen on the new pieces. And the tokens themselves – thicker and heavier than in the past – needed steam-powered presses to strike them and often to apply thread milling to their edges, a finish that had become popular when used on the regal halfpennies of 1799. It is worth noting that although the images on the tokens just described suggest a booming economy and regular weekly wage packets, a number were struck as workhouse tokens for use by those pitched into poverty by the needs of capitalism. Those tokens were handed out as payment for menial work. Recipients could spend them at specified local shops on bread and other essentials. The shopkeeper usually had to take the tokens back to the workhouse to exchange them for cash.

The influence of regal twopenny and penny coins can be seen in the general appearance of many early 19th century tokens, which are thicker and heavier than 18th century issues. Pictorially they record the industrialisation of Britain and the dominance of mining and metalworking industries. Stylistically they lack the artistic spontaneity of earlier times, preferring simpler images and larger lettering.

Not to scale

Early 19th Century Tokens

Not to scale

Countermarked Spanish pillar dollar or piece of eight.

Obverse and reverse of token issued by Rackhams Circulating Library.

The influence of the regal cartwheel penny can be seen around the thickened edges of this attractive token.

Obverse and reverse of Bank of England silver token for 18d, dated 1812.

Not to scale

Conspicuously absent from the story of tokens in the 19th century were the collectors who had proved such enthusiastic buyers before 1799. Perhaps the utilitarian designs lacked appeal; perhaps the melting away of collectors left little incentive for the makers to turn out miniature works of art. They did produce plenty of tokens for general circulation, but these were used primarily as much needed small change.

Equally surprising is that whereas up to 20,000 small traders in England and Wales issued tokens in the 17th century, only a fraction of that number did so in the 19th century. The few that issued tokens – drapers, grocers, mercers and the like – tended to prefer halfpennies and farthings rather than the pennies used by larger companies. As previously explained, there was little call for tokens in 17th century Scotland, thanks to a plentiful supply of copper coinage in that country. In the 18th century Scottish issues were almost all town tokens. But in the 19th century privately issued lead tokens appeared in fairly large numbers, as well as some Scottish copper halfpennies.

Inevitably the 19th century token boom attracted attention from counterfeiters who initially produced lightweight pieces issued by copper companies that simply did not exist. Later they circulated considerably underweight halfpennies, as well as pennies bearing patriotic slogans and phrases such as *For General Circulation* in expectation that the public might take them as official, even regal issues. Many complaints against these tricksters led eventually to the banning of copper tokens in 1817.

War and rumours of French invasion caused hoarding of gold and silver on a huge scale in Britain before Napoleon was finally defeated at Waterloo. The Royal Mint, in the throes of a move to new premises, and still using antiquated machinery, could not keep pace with demand for replacement silver coins. As a temporary measure the government decided on an emergency issue of silver tokens. The Mint used Spanish pieces of eight captured when towns were looted in the Peninsula War, or taken at sea from Spanish ships, and countermarked them with a small bust of George III stamped on the neck of the Spanish king. (In a single spectacular engagement at sea a Spanish treasure ship carrying silver worth 3,000,000 Spanish dollars fell into English hands in 1804).

Almost two and a half million of these unusual pieces went into circulation with an official value of four shillings and ninepence. But in a matter of weeks the scheme backfired when speculators discovered that they could buy un-stamped Spanish dollars at four shillings and eightpence. Forging the countermark proved all too easy and a large number of counterfeits began to circulate. The Mint switched to a different punch, but that countermark was also soon copied. Ironically it required a private token manufacturer, Matthew Boulton of the Soho Mint, Birmingham, to rescue the situation. He offered to use his powerful steam presses to convert Spanish dollars to English money with a single strike that effaced the Spanish impression and struck a new English piece at the same time. These handsome Bank of England dollars, valued at five shillings, were soon in circulation, though on some of them faint traces of Spanish lettering remained.

I should point out that counterfeiting remained a hanging offence at this time, and those who put forged marks on the Spanish king's neck risked their own necks. Between 1805 and 1818, 207 people - including several women - went to the gallows for this offence. After 1825 the sentence was reduced to 14 years' transportation.

The silver bullion price continued to rise and Bank of England dollars began to disappear into melting pots once again until, on 11 March, 1811, the Government issued the following statement:-

Whereas the price of silver has risen so much since the first issue of Bank Dollar Tokens at five shillings each, as now to make them worth more [when] sold as bullion, it has been found expedient ... that an additional value in relation to their intrinsic value be now assigned to them. The Government and the Bank of England therefore give notice that from henceforth Bank Dollar Tokens will be received at the rate of five shillings and sixpence each.

In the same year the Bank of England issued two more token values – for three-and-sixpence and one-and-sixpence. They went into circulation in July 1811, but by September the Government was obliged to announce that:-

Counterfeits of the three-shilling Bank Token are in circulation. Their appearance is much whiter, and they sound very dull when rung. They are of copper, thinly plated and worth about a penny. On the whole they are executed nearly as well as those issued by the Bank, and it is much to be lamented that the execution of the Bank Token has admitted of so early and easy a counterfeit. Persons to whom [they are offered] will do a public service by endeavouring to trace the quarter from whence they first came into circulation.

Public exasperation at the continuing shortage of silver coins had by that time pushed many provincial banks and not a few factory owners into issuing their own private silver tokens. In Scotland the practice grew up of buying-in Spanish and sometimes French silver coins, readily available on the London bullion market, then cutting them into fractions as necessary, and stamping private countermarks on them for sums ranging from one-and-eightpence to six shillings. The issuers had to pitch the declared face value slightly higher than the intrinsic silver value to avoid the melting pot.

Silver Tokens

Provincial silver tokens were produced from Spanish bullion. The issuers had to keep the weight low enough to deter melting down but high enough to satisfy users of token money.

Base Metal

Many worn Georgian coppers were put back into circulation in mid-Victorian times carrying countermarked advertising. This one was reused by "Lloyd's Weekly Newspaper".

19th Century Tokens of Essex

Some examples of a vast series of 19th century Walthamstow tokens.

Not to scale

In England tokens as attractive as the coppers of the late 18th century, but in silver, and for values ranging from sixpence up to three shillings, were circulated by county banks, town corporations, factory owners and others. They often carried declarations that they had been *issued for the convenience of trade.*

By 1816 the Royal Mint had moved from the Tower of London to a new site on Tower Hill where modern steam-powered minting machinery at last made possible the minting of all the coins the nation required. Ironically the silver coins of 1816 – crowns, halfcrowns, shillings and sixpences – were all tokens, having an intrinsic silver content substantially below their face value. It took until 1821 for the new Mint to perform a similar job in supplying enough new pennies, halfpennies and farthings to end the need for copper tokens, which had been declared illegal by an Act of Parliament on 1817 and which gradually withered away as the public lost faith and interest in them, preferring to rely instead on the Government's declared but rarely tested promise to pay bearers on demand the face value of its now plentiful regal coppers.

One beneficial side effect of a circulating token to a trader was that it advertised the name and location of his premises at no real cost, since the medium was the message. The only other obvious forms of advertising available in mid-Victorian England were printed handbills, announcements in the columns of local newspapers, or bills pasted up on the flat surfaces of gable-end walls where they might catch the public's eye. All three incurred a not inconsiderable outlay. But some traders' eyes were drawn to the bright new regal coppers that had by then replaced tokens. Why not take a few hundred farthings or halfpennies down to a local workshop and pay to have them stamped with the name and address of the business?

This happened increasingly during the 1850s, though much of the countermarking was carried out by factory and mine owners who used such coins as *truck money*, which will be discussed in another chapter. The man who countermarked the greatest number of coins of the realm in this way was probably Edward Lloyd, proprietor of Lloyd's Weekly Newspaper, but many other firms followed his lead until the practice was forbidden in 1853.

Famously one firm that found a loophole in the law was the manufacturer of Pears' Soap. The company imported a large quantity of bronze coins from France, Spain and Luxembourg and countermarked them with adverts for its products before slipping them into British circulation. A prohibition against the importing of base metal foreign money curtailed the practice in 1887. After that date some firms found another loophole by stamping their adverts only on pre-1860s copper coins, which had been largely replaced by bronze issues after 1860. When supplies of old coppers dried up as the Mint destroyed them, the final phases of this unusual form of advertising included pasting coin-sized paper labels on the surfaces of coins, together with giving away cardboard coins similar to the educational cut-outs already discussed.

Identifying Finds In The Field

Look closely at all old and worn coppers; faded countermarks on them are easily missed. Large numbers of worn 19th century tokens turn up, proof that unlike the earlier collectors' pieces of the 18th century, these later tokens circulated widely.

Recommended Further Reading

British Copper Tokens 1811-1820 by Withers P. & B., Galata, 1999.

Chapter 9

Unofficial Farthings & Other 19th Century Advertising Issues

In 1813, Napoleon Bonaparte called the British "a nation of shopkeepers"; but he was obliged to eat his words just two years later at Waterloo, where English, Scottish, Welsh and Irish infantrymen and gunners taught him that the British were still a militaristic nation, as formidable on land as at sea. In fairness Old Boney had no statistical evidence on which to base his claim; he spoke with that same ignorance of our shopping and shop-keeping habits displayed by officials at the British Royal Mint when, during various periods between 1820 and 1870, they grossly underestimated the nation's requirements for small change.

It has already been demonstrated that the greatest need for low denomination coinage came from society's poorer sections; that while a duke and duchess might comfortably get by with a jingle of silver and gold in pocket or purse, a labourer and his missus needed pennies, halfpennies and especially farthings in plentiful numbers to buy their daily subsistence needs.

Our present-day decimal monetary system has no fractional pence; we don't require them. But in 1820 four oysters could be had for a penny, and a state of dead drunkenness achieved for 2d. Farthings oiled the wheels of such everyday transactions for folk who could not afford the whole penny.

To describe the British as mere shopkeepers was clearly misleading; we were in the throes of the Industrial Revolution and most of those who were not ironmasters or mill owners worked in the factories and mills of such entrepreneurs. But by 1820 we were well on the way to becoming a nation of addicted shoppers. The High Streets and market places of all cities and towns boasted a wide range of retail premises. Indeed, even the smallest town probably had three or four grocers, clothiers, tea dealers and wine merchants. Customers of every social standing had begun to shop with discernment, on the lookout for bargains and/or quality in everything from tallow candles to winter overcoats. Shopkeepers who encounter potential customers empowered with freedom of choice can respond in three ways: they can reduce prices, improve the quality of goods stocked, or they can advertise. Most took option three and spent extravagantly on handbills, wall posters, and even classified or semi-display advertising in local newspapers.

The latter course, although guaranteed to bring one's wares to the attention of a large number of potential buyers, was an expensive means of generating custom. A weekly newspaper with a

Unofficial 19th Century Issues

Richard Owen, Caernarvon, linen and woollen draper and tailor circa 1837
26mm round, brass.

T.J. Williams, Denbigh, general draper, tailor and outfitter circa 1868-1899 32mm round, brass.

Benjamin Littler, Rhyl, grocer and dealer in sundries circa 1865-1868 29mm round, white metal.

Not to scale

Unofficial 19th Century Issues

Korner & Co., Cardiff, shirt maker etc. circa 1870-1890 24mm round, brass.

William Covington, Swansea, tailor, draper and outfitter circa 1858 20mm round, brass.

William Hasquencort, Swansea, hatter and hairdresser, 21mm round, brass.

John Harris Conway, Abergavenny, grocer and tea dealer circa 1844-1871 22mm round, brass.

Thomas Perkins, Chepstow, grocer and tea dealer circa 1843-1876 22mm round, brass.

Alfred Taylor, Newport, Mon, merchant tailor circa 1868-1901 28mm round, brass.

Not to scale

The need to promote sales in the face of stiff competition encouraged businesses of all types to issue tokens imitating regal coinage while declaring their advertising messages to Victorian consumers. These examples give a flavour of the huge series of unofficial farthings and advertising tokens that flooded Britain in the 19th century.

Not to scale

19th Century Advertising Tokens

Not to scale

19th Century Advertising Tokens

Not to scale

cover price of 2d in 1835 actually cost the purchaser 9d when the savage 7d in Newspaper Stamp Duty was added. Popular agitation forced the government to reduce the duty to 1d in 1836, but even that amount often doubled the 1d price the publisher wished to charge. And the group of shoppers least likely to shell out 2d for a newspaper were the very people who used farthings most often as change.

The minting and issuing of tradesmen's tokens had been declared illegal by the British government in 1818, bringing to an end a 20-year period of prolific penny and halfpenny token production. Inevitably, the shortage of farthings experienced after 1818 turned the thoughts of many retailers to private issues once again. Coincidentally the term price ticket had become current in retailing at about that time; it was used when referring to small paper or cardboard stickers attached to items displayed in shop windows and carrying details of size, price and the shopkeeper's name. Emboldened by necessity, some retailers hit on the notion of metal tickets, in shape and size identical to farthings, even (in some cases) bearing the monarch's head; but they showed no denomination, nor any pledge to exchange them for regal coinage. Instead they carried blatant advertising for the retailer - his name, address, type of business, and a message providing positive information about the goods on sale. Issuers usually insisted on referring to them as advertising tickets to avoid prosecution; at the same time they handed them out in change whenever tills ran short of farthings. Assurances to customers that they could return to the shop at a later date with the advertising ticket and use it as a pledge for one farthing - and that other tradesmen in the town had agreed to accept the circular disc as a farthing whenever the need arose - encouraged the public to take to what were, in effect, unofficial farthings, as eagerly as they had taken to tokens many times in the past.

Official reaction to unofficial farthings amounted to a few grumbles but a blind eye. In response, increasing numbers of traders began to pour tokens into their tills, often requesting the engraver to keep as closely as possible to the obverse design on Victoria's Young Head farthings of 1838-1859. Prince Albert's head also made its appearance on token farthings, but another image became far more popular after 1851. The Great Exhibition of that year celebrated the industrial and imperial might of Britain. Conceived by the Prince Consort, the mammoth event took place in a specially constructed Crystal Palace erected in Hyde Park. It housed more than 13,000 exhibits of ingenuity, artistry and invention, which were viewed by over 6,000,000 visitors to the exhibition during that year. Profits from the event provided funds for public works such as the Albert Hall, the Science Museum, the National History Museum and the Victoria and Albert Museum. At the same time the exhibition provided retailers who wished to promote their businesses as up-to-the-minute and thoroughly modern with an instantly recognizable image to place on their unofficial farthing issues. The Crystal Palace became second only to Queen Victoria's bust as a popular subject for the obverses of these tokens.

Responding to officialdom's apparent willingness to allow tokens to circulate as private money, numbers of traders in larger cities and towns cooperated to introduce farthings bearing legends such as "For General Circulation", which could be used as money over a wide area in many retail outlets. Irish and Scottish merchants now often declared a value of one farthing on their issues, while traders in England introduced larger denominations up to several shillings, although their tokens were almost all stamped in either copper or brass. What shop owners could get away with encouraged others having a need for small change to follow suit. Soon farthing-sized tea checks, coal tallies, theatre passes, ferry and omnibus tickets, toll bridge passes, public house checks for dominoes, cards, bagatelle and skittles could be found passing locally as farthings in numerous cities and towns. Long after 1870, when adequate supplies of regal farthings made shopkeepers' unofficial farthings redundant, huge numbers of metal tickets circulated as part of the advertising mania that swept Britain in the late 19th century.

The English traders, shopkeepers, merchants and others most often represented on unofficial farthings included tea dealers, clothiers, wine and spirit merchants, oil and colourmen, grocers and tobacconists. In Ireland, where use was quite widespread, silk mercers and linen drapers were well represented alongside tea dealers, wine and spirit merchants and grocers. But beyond Dublin very few unofficial farthings carried Queen Victoria's image. However, she was often seen on the Dublin issues of tea merchants, drapers and tavern keepers.

In Scotland private issues were much less common, their places often taken by general issues of Glasgow or Edinburgh tradesmen, bearing such phrases as "Commerce Token" or "Glasgow Retailers Token", and a stated redeemable value of "One Farthing". Some interesting but scarce examples turn up north of the border, including pieces issued by medical practitioners and fancy goods merchants. Throughout Britain wide variations in the appearance of Queen Victoria's bust can be found, although most often the monarch faces right and she wears her hair in the style depicted on Young Head regal farthings. The metal favoured was copper, again in imitation of the regal coin, although a few examples are known in brass, pewter, and even lead.

As with 17th century traders' tokens, interest in unofficial farthings comes as much from genealogists as from paranumismatists. The wealth of information squeezed onto a typical token of those times - the name of the business proprietor; the trading address; the nature of the business; sometimes the addresses of other branches and the names or initials of sons, wives, daughters; occasionally an engraved illustration of the building or examples of stock on sale - make them highly desirable to historians. Each piece adds up to a durable record and a rich source of local social history. Further excitement is added to seeking specimens by the knowledge that hitherto unrecorded examples turn up regularly as fieldwalkers' finds, as discoveries at boot sales, in coin dealers' miscellaneous departments, tucked away in old button boxes, or even still in use as counters for board games.

Identifying Finds In The Field

Any copper or brass piece about the size of a modern 1p, and bearing a Young Head Queen Victoria image, is likely to be an unofficial farthing if the reverse does not depict a seated Britannia. The lettering on other advertising tokens and the like should leave little doubt about their purpose.

Recommended Further Reading

Unofficial Farthings: 1820-1870 by Bell R.C., Seaby, 1974.

Chapter 10

Pub Checks

In the decades following the introduction of George III's copper farthings in 1821, and his pennies and halfpennies four years later, England enjoyed an abundance of small change for the first time since the departure of the Romans almost one and a half thousand years earlier. One might expect at this juncture that the roles of tokens, tallies and their ilk would begin to wither away; and that legal coppers would soon become the only small pieces of metal found in pockets and purses. But this was not the case. In fact, people devised dozens of new or modified roles for paranumismatica as 19th century social, economic and political life picked up pace, diversity and complexity. To use a writer's analogy, I would argue that tokens, tallies, checks, counters, chips, jettons and countermarks served the same roles in relation to money that pronouns serve in relation to nouns. (For readers whose schooling occurred post-1970, I'll remind you that those little words I, you, he, she, it, we, they, me, him, her, us, them, mine, yours, its, theirs, and a few more, are all pronouns. We use them in speech and writing to avoid repetition of nouns, and for speed and ease in communication. Try speaking or writing without using pronouns and you'll soon appreciate their importance.) Let's look at one small paranumismatic classification – pub checks – and see how they functioned in relation to money.

What did pub checks look like? Brass discs a little smaller than a Victorian halfpenny, with the name of the issuing pub on the obverse, usually with the name of the landlord and a value - 1d, 3d, 4d were the most likely denominations. A substantial minority had an obverse image showing either the pub's sign or the pub itself. Reverses repeated the value, often had the word "Check", and sometimes had an image depicting a man playing nine-pin bowls, a man playing billiards, or an illustration of a bagatelle board. The words "Bowling Alley", "Billiards Room", or "Bagatelle Room" also occasionally appeared. Their early history probably connects with the locally-made "leaden money" mentioned so often in reference to public houses, taverns and inns in Elizabethan times and earlier; but these die-struck brass checks came mainly from Birmingham workshops. The pubs of Wales used checks in huge numbers and almost all their orders went to west Midlands makers. London landlords and those in northern industrial cities and towns may have turned to local die-casters for supplies.

Some paranumismatic authorities suggest that the arrival of hoards of Irish labourers via Liverpool sparked the introduction of the checks because Dublin pubs used checks before they became popular in England and Wales. It is argued that buying checks in prepayment for pints of beer would have speeded service in busy bars and helped the landlord control the contents of his tills. I can imagine thirsty Irish labourers appreciating faster service; but the notion of a labourer of any nationality handing over beer money in prepayment seems highly unlikely.

Others have suggested that the advertising function of pub checks was their most important role; that landlords gave them away at certain times to attract customers. Free beer or free use of skittle alleys and similar facilities is laudable and probably occurred on some occasions; but a third and more complex function, devised in part to get around gambling laws, seems much more plausible. Old men interviewed in the 1970s and asked about pub checks and skittle alleys in the 1920s and 30s explained the use of the checks as follows.

A game of skittles, snooker or bagatelle was arranged by the landlord who charged each player a small sum for hire of the equipment – sixpence is often mentioned, but the amount may have been less

Welsh Pub Checks

QUEENS HOTEL, CAERPHILLY 1d 26mm, round, brass circa 1896-1901.

MORLAIS CASTLE, High Street, Merthyr Tydfil M. Williams 3d 29mm, round, brass circa 1876-1878.

SHIP & CASTLE, St. Marys Street, Cardiff R.Howell 3d 26mm round/brass W. Blatchers' Improved Patent Tables [bagatelle table depicted] 1 door from Bull St., Temple Row, Birmingham circa 1857/8.

London pub checks rarely included pictorial designs, but attractive typefaces - as here - were a common feature on these Victorian relics.

London pub check for 4d. At the time of writing "The Prince of Orange", Lower Rd, Rotherhithe, is under the threat of demolition.

Pub check for skittles.

Refreshment check for a pub concert.

Not to scale

in Victorian times. If 20 players participated the landlord provided 20 checks as prizes. Each check could be exchanged for a pint of beer or other beverage equal to the amount stamped on the check. Thus, if beer was 4d a pint, the landlord earned 2d from each entrant, in addition to any profit on selling a pint. And his checks, bearing the emblem of his pub, could not be used to buy beer from rival establishments. With no money changing hands as prizes, the gambling laws were only slightly bent by these games of skill.

It sounds right; it demonstrates the versatility of paranumismatica; and it should alert us to the fact that culture, especially working class culture in which so many small pieces of brass, copper and lead circulated, was invariably complex. At some pubs, especially in large towns where the drinkers crowded the bars as well as the skittle alleys and other facilities on pay nights, the landlord often engaged local talent to sing or play music for the benefit of his customers. The rooms set aside for such pleasures were the early manifestations of what evolved into music halls and gaiety theatres in the late 19th century. Pub checks also evolved to meet this need, becoming admission tickets, with an element of the price at the door returned to customers in the form of a brass disc bearing instruction for use such as "3d To Be Spent On Refreshments The Same Evening As This Check Received".

Among several other ways in which the versatility of pub checks met local needs was as rewards to employees who perhaps worked overtime at short notice. A factory owner might have purchased a number of the checks from a publican some time earlier, to be given out when he wanted to thank his men for their efforts to complete a particularly important order.

Identifying Finds In The Field

If a pub name is engraved on any small coin-like find, you have probably recovered a pub check in one of its various forms. Local trade directories can be used to pinpoint the sites of vanished pubs, which make excellent places to carry out searches for more checks. Many pub checks were later pressed into service as counters for board games, so they can turn up in old game boxes.

Recommended Further Reading

Tavern Tokens In Wales by Todd N.B., National Museum of Wales, 1980.

Chapter 11

Work, Play & Games

A look At Educational Coins, Toy Money & Gaming Tokens from Victorian & Edwardian times

Twelve pence one shilling
Eighteen pence one-and-six
Thirty pence two-and-six
Sixty pence five shillings
Two hundred and forty pence....

Well, if you don't know the answer to the last line you must be a child of the Decimal Age and quite satisfied with 100 pence to the pound. Things were different in my infancy. I certainly recall having to learn the alphabet backwards or face physical abuse; and I can just recall cardboard cut-out farthings, halfpennies, pennies, threepences, sixpences, shillings, florins and halfcrowns with which I had to work out how much change I'd get from a pound note if sent on an errand to buy groceries costing thirteen-and-nine-pence-three-farthings.

Victorian children had the benefit of more realistic token money, made from metal and with both obverse and reverse stamped, unlike my cardboard memories, which were most certainly uniface. I recall finding my first Victorian example about 20 years ago while clearing an old sand pit in the garden of an 18th century house: a copper piece with twelve raised dots and a young head - no, infant head - and bearing the inscription *12 pence make 1 shilling*. I'm sure it was smaller than a modern 5p; and I thought at the time that it might be a dolls' house accessory. Later research revealed my find came from a range of educational toy money going up to *2 Half-Sovereigns Make One Pound*, and manufactured in the 1840s and later by S.G. Onions & Co for use in the same way as my infant school's cardboard money worked a century later. The children's tiny fingers touched the dots as they counted aloud to drum home the arithmetic.

Another small coin that I wrongly assumed to be a toy turned up during floorboard repairs at the same property. It must have become lost when it fell into the gap between two boards many years earlier. I thought I'd found an old halfpenny until I rubbed away a coating of greasy dust and saw what looked like silver beneath; but the edges of the coin were decidedly dull. I had discovered one of those fairly common bi-metallic coins with Queen Victoria's young head and a legend reading *Victoria Reg: One Penny Model*. The reverse had a figure "1" at its centre.

The first fruits of later research revealed that the central insert is not silver at all, but white metal (a

How to play without losing money. The following are all examples of gaming counters from days gone by.

George IV crown.

Prince of Wales half sovereign.

To Hanover.

Don't lose your temper.

Nuremburg Spielmarken.

Five Imitation Spade Guineas

With full Latin abbreviation.

In Memory of the Good Old Days.

With advertising on reverse.

More reverse advertising.

John Sainsbury felt his shop
deserved obverse exposure.

tin alloy) with a convincing silvery appearance. The coins were first made in 1848 by a well-known Birmingham engraver and medal maker named Joseph Moore. He did not have the toy market in mind at the time. Rather he was suggesting to the government of the day that the weights of low denomination coins such as pennies could be greatly reduced by the use of lighter white metal inserts, thereby saving money on copper, which was rising in price at the time. He also stressed the benefits of reducing the burden of heavy coppers in pockets and purses. Moore used the term "Model" in the sense of a *proposed plan* rather than in the sense of *a miniature version* such as a model aircraft that I had in mind. The government turned his model down, but the general public liked it so much they began to use Moore's pennies as currency, which explains why so many lost specimens turn up today.

The engraver might have faced prosecution for counterfeiting had not that word "Model" appeared on his pennies. In fact, the Royal Mint issued an official statement stressing that Model pennies were not legal tender. Nevertheless, Moore went on to sell large numbers of them, as well as many of his much smaller bi-metallic fractional farthings and other strange denominations, which found a ready market as toy money. Incidentally, the size of the regal standard penny was later reduced quite considerably with the bun penny issue of 1860.

I've never found any examples of what paranumismatists refer to as "imitation toy coins", although I've seen them in dealers' trays. They differ from the bi-metallics just discussed in two important ways: they are not bi-metallic; and they do not bear the word "Model". In fact, many of them look almost identical to the full-sized version of the coins they imitate; they are so close, in fact, we might wonder how their makers avoided prosecution for counterfeiting. Well, they did it by coining only Lilliputian-sized coins, usually 13mm or less in diameter, which were obviously imitations.

Many firms made them, but it is the work of Nuremburg jetton makers Lauer that is most often encountered in Britain. Lauer imitated many of the coins of Victoria, Edward VII, and even George V, often including the firm's name, or the terms "Counter" and *Imitation* within the legend on the coins as an added safeguard against prosecution. The metals all looked authentic even though they employed brass for gold, white-plated iron for silver, and copper for bronze. In dealers' trays you'll see Young Head, Gothic Head, Jubilee Head, Diamond Jubilee Head and Old Head Lauer miniatures of Victoria, each no more than 13mm in diameter, and at very reasonable prices for such tiny works of art.

We tend to forget in this couch-potato-and-flat-screen world the importance of games in Victorian homes. Songs around the parlour piano, charades around the fireside, and board games of all sorts around the family table sum up how the average 19th century family spent many of its leisure hours. Whether playing for amusement or for small stakes, keeping track of winners and losers provided an important part of the ritual. That's why so many gaming pieces from the Victorian age have come down to us. They were used in scoring; to mark positions on boards; to serve as token money when a flutter on the roll of a dice or the turn of a card would add to the excitement. And how much more thrilling this was when the stakes had the appearance of gold without the risk of losing a fortune!

Before 1750 the market for gaming counters relied on imports of German *spielmarken* from Nuremberg. Birmingham began to compete in the late 18th century, starting a long-lasting series of counters that imitated the gold coinage of Queen Anne and George III. They were usually of the correct size for a guinea (24mm-27mm) but were struck in brass instead of gold. They had bungled inscriptions and incorrect dates, again as a safeguard against counterfeiting charges, and perhaps also to avoid falling foul of laws against gambling for money. Early imitations featured the crowned and ornate shield reverse, but the ornate shield gave way to a pointed shield resembling the contemporary garden spade. It was widely known as a spade reverse....very appropriate for card playing. Wording on the reverse had several variations including: *In Memory Of The Good Old Days; The Olden Times; Honi Soit Qui Mal Y Pense*; and *M B F ET H REX F D B ET L D S R I A T E T E* (Latin initials that translate as "King of Great Britain, France and Ireland, Defender of the Faith, Duke of Brunswick and Luneburg, High Treasurer and Elector of the Holy Roman Empire").

Many pieces were holed when manufactured, or later, to facilitate counting and for hanging on strings. Production continued for about 20 years, until regal sovereigns replaced regal guineas. However, in the 1800s imitation spade guineas got a new lease of life, thanks to the Counterfeit Medal Act. They clearly now had an obsolete design and an obsolete value, so could not be confused in any way with coin of the realm. Production re-commenced and continued generally until the 1930s. Apart from use as gaming counters, many appeared as fobs on watch-chains, and they were often used as throw-away money in theatre pantomimes. Their popularity induced many traders to advertise a variety of goods and services on the counters. I've seen quite a few, but I was startled to learn that specialists in this minute segment of paranumismatics have catalogued more than 1,000 variations, including advertising and non-advertising types.

Another frequently encountered survivor from the period is the "To Hanover" counter with a copy of a Queen Victoria sovereign as its obverse and a reverse depicting a crowned horseman accompanied

Working on mental arithmetic. These Victorian teaching aids familiarised tiny tots with the harsh realities of poverty and wealth. They were made by Onions & Co, circa 1840.

Moore's bi-metallic "Model Penny" turned down by the Government but welcomed by the public, circa 1844.

Moore's delightful model 2 shillings.

Even more attractive, his bi-metallic crown.

The name of the Nuremburg maker Lauer appears with the obverse legend on this toy halfpenny. On the reverse the denomination is spelt "penni".

Moore's one-sixteenth scale model farthing.

Toy sovereign of Edward VII dated 1902.

CM

by a three-headed dragon and the legend: *To Hanover*. Some also bear the date 1837, which is not the year of manufacture, but the year Victoria's uncle, the unpopular Duke of Cumberland, left England to become Hanover's monarch on the death of William IV. As a male, the duke took precedence over female Victoria under German law. Production of these counters continued long after the affair lost its topicality.

"Jacks", another name for gaming counters, led to these tokens becoming known as "Cumberland Jacks". Most were used as gaming counters; but incidents of them passing as forgeries reached the ears of authority following the reintroduction of the St George and Dragon reverse on regal coinage in 1871. It made the "To Hanover" counters look so much like real sovereigns they sometimes duped the unsuspecting. But the Counterfeit Medal Act of 1883 put a stop to their production. Collectors have catalogued over a 100 variations including obverses with *Victoria Queen Of Great Britain*; *Victoria Regina*; and *H.M.G.M. Queen Victoria*.

The Prince of Wales model sovereign, issued from 1842 until the 1870s, proved another popular gaming counter. Its obverse showed Victoria's head, but the reverse has the emblems of the Prince of Wales and the legend *The Prince of Wales Model Sovrn*. Half sovereigns of this type seem even more common, often found paired with a "To Hanover" sovereign. Another well-known gaming counter of the period depicts a card player on the obverse, with the words *Keep Your Temper* on the reverse.

Identifying Finds In The Field

I suspect that many lost specimens of the tiniest toy money items mentioned in this chapter have slipped unnoticed past the eyes of mudlarks and excavators. Losses wherever children gathered in Victorian times must have been high. Many examples await discovery, as my finds did, down cracks and crevices in old houses. Dealers may already have scoured button boxes and the miscellaneous trays of other dealers; but small items like these are easily missed.

Recommended Further Reading

A Dictionary of British Metallic Tickets, Checks, Medalets, Tallies and Counters, 1788-1910 by Hawkins, R.N.P., London, 1989
Toy Coins by de Sola Rogers, D.J., 1990; Galata Print
Imitation Spade Guineas by Magnay D., 1997
To Hanover Counters by Bryce Nelson W., 1998

Chapter 12

Market Traders' Tallies

In the 1890s refrigerators were almost unknown and most food retailing was in the hands of small shopkeepers and market traders. More than a quarter of all fresh food – vegetables, meat, fish – went on sale at local markets once or twice a week. The trader had to hope he would sell-out by the end of the day and not find himself obliged to off-load too much on the half-starved unemployed who hung around at closing time desperate for bargains.

Getting fresh produce of all kinds into town and city markets so that selling could commence as soon as daylight and regulations permitted, demanded planning, timing, some occasional petty bribery, and a great deal of skill. The stallholder's day probably began around 4 or 5am with a battle to carve his way through a crush of barrows, boxes, carts, horses, lorries and a higher level of bureaucracy at a wholesale market where his bids and buying decisions largely determined whether or not he made a decent profit come closing time. One way to speed the process a little came in handling his purchases. A crate of apples, a box of haddock, a tray of pigs' trotters transferred more speedily from wholesaler's stacks to the back of the trader's van if crate, box or tray went with the raw food. The wholesaler concurred because he, too, felt rushed off his feet. But not so rushed that he would risk a good container without demanding a deposit at least equal to its purchase price. Therein lies the genesis of market traders' tallies.

In the Guildhall Library, London is housed a superb collection of paintings and old photographs depicting the City in ages past. I recently looked closely at several images of Billingsgate Market up to 200 years ago. In Georgian times there were no wholesalers in fish apart from the fishermen themselves. One lively painting has on the right of the scene a group of fish salesmen about to set off around the neighbouring counties with some of the morning's catch. Fish boxes are not in evidence. The fish have been pitched directly into saddle baskets slung across the backs of mules. They probably received a covering of seaweed and, in winter, a few bits of broken ice alongside them in the basket, and then off they trotted down the bridleways that led into Essex, Hertfordshire and further inland. The mule driver owned his own saddlery so all monies that changed hands between boat owner and salesman paid for fish. And the cottage housewife in Hertfordshire who bought her fresh herring at her front-door later in the day probably carried it indoors on her own plate.

Another collection is available to market tally researchers: the Neal Archive, an old ledger that records the work of London die-cutters and tally makers, Charles Neal & Son, between 1948 and 1974. The firm made numerous tallies for market traders and wholesalers, including several from Billingsgate. The family had done similar work since the 1840s. Although the ledger only records work done in the 20th century, evidence from dated finds of this company's (and others') earlier work suggests few major changes in tally design over more than a century.

A third source of information on early tallies used in the Billingsgate area comes from finds on the Thames foreshores, close to the old fish market, of many of those enigmatic lead tallies or tokens, often bearing no more than initials and the occasional flower petals or geometric motifs, that you can see vividly displayed in the chapter on Medieval Tokens.

Using that albeit incomplete evidence, we can conjecture that up to the early 19th century few if any market traders' tallies were used in London, or anywhere in Britain. The Victorian advent of die-cut-

These photographs show an assortment of Victorian market tallies, some used by wholesalers, others by farmers sending their produce to local markets in their own containers. Note the variety of shapes such as the pierced examples. They clearly indicated value, ownership, and that all are the work of die cutters R. Neal of London.

Not to scale

*Obverse - Typical Neal workmanship in the unusual shape,
unusual piercing, and bold lettering.
Reverse - Figures occupy most of the surface.*

*Obverse - More conventional piercing can be seen on the large tally.
Reverse - Unusual numerals, probably for a 10 shilling deposit.*

*Obverse - A Birmingham fish merchant - a long way
from Billingsgate. Reverse - The value of 2/-.*

Not to scale

ters workshops willing to take orders for relatively small numbers of pieces in copper, brass, pewter and tin must have coincided with technological changes in the structure of food distribution. Something happened to create a need for tallies bearing the names of wholesalers and traders, the locations of their businesses, the amount of money deposited for use of various containers, and – perhaps as a security measure, or a means of identification in poor light – the piercing of very many tallies with oddly-shaped holes. A browse through the approximately 700 tallies, tool checks and similar pieces illustrated (by pencil rubbings of obverse and reverse) in the Neal Archive reveals the following facts.

Work was undertaken for London traders in Spitalfields Market, Stratford Market, Covent Garden Market, Borough Market, Billingsgate Market and the LNER Potato Market near King's Cross.

More than 90% of the tallies were manufactured in brass.

Most of the tallies were about the size of a present-day 50p, but in a variety of shapes including round, oval, square, scalloped, octagonal, oblong, heart, triangular, loaf, shield and others too complex to describe here.

The largest lettering, usually occupying most of one side, gave the amount to be deposited - anything from 6d to 20 shillings (one was noted for £2).

The manufacturing instructions included orders to pierce various shapes through more than half of the tallies. Many piercings required the surname letter of the company's name. Other piercings called for stars, circles, squares and unconventional shapes. The piercings might have been for attachment purposes, or for stringing the tallies during storage, or for purposes now unknown.

Quantities on each order range from 100 to 500 pieces. Some are obviously repeat orders, which include phrases such as *same as in 1939* and other references to past business.

Most of what is recorded above would apply to the business and the order books of diesinkers in London, Birmingham and elsewhere in Britain from the 19th to the mid-20th century.

Identifying Finds In The Field

Begin with lots of photographs and descriptions of market tallies found in your locality. Follow up with searches of Kelly's and other Victorian – Edwardian trade directories. Make lists of engravers and diesinkers. Look out for their advertisements in appropriate trade publications. When you make finds look for the die-maker's name as well as the name of the market trader.

Recommended Further Reading

Glasgow Market Tallies by Macmillan A.T., 1997.
Birmingham Market Tokens by Whitmore J., 1995.

Chapter 13

Tokens & Tallies In 19th & Early 20th Century Agriculture

The hectic story of tokens during the industrialisation of Georgian and Victorian cities and towns makes it easy to forget that in many parts of rural Britain economic and social life drifted along at much the same pace that it had moved in Elizabethan times. Hundreds of village communities remained untouched by the Age of Steam, and their inhabitants would have felt quite at home within the pages of a Thomas Hardy or George Elliott novel. In such communities, where every man knew his neighbour, and the local squire held the purse strings, farm labourers probably still used plenty of lead tallies in their day-to-day dealings with each other, whether playing games, or putting in a few hours' work on another man's plot, or keeping account of what they owed the landlord at the village pub, with reckonings to be settled in coin of the realm on the one or two occasions each year when wages were paid. But in eastern and south-eastern England a new breed of gentleman farmer had evolved; one who appreciated the economic opportunities offered by threshing machines, steam ploughs and the generous application of fertiliser to boost crop yields with the aid of science. Such methods called for a different kind of labour force; not tied to the land and depending on the owner in every season; but casual, living off-farm, yet available for hire at a few hours' notice when needed at planting and harvest times. The only problem an independent labour force presents to an employer lies in the possibility that the labourers might exercise their independence and take a few days off during times when their muscle power is most urgently required. Therein lies the more potent power of tallies and tokens: they can discipline the most unruly of casual labourers and force them to work at times and at paces to suit the landowner's needs.

In the 1950s, as a pre-teenager addicted to Wills' Woodbines, I did casual potato-picking work to earn the price of a few days' smokes on two East Yorkshire farms during one hectic "spud-bashing" season. On the first job the farmer paid half-a-crown for a full day's picking, 8 am to 6 pm, with a 30-minute lunch break. Each picker had a stint, a length along the rows marked off by two stakes and between which he/she had to pick all the potatoes each time the tractor ran along the row and grubbed up the crop. At this distance in time I'm willing to confess that most of my day was spent in devising methods of doing as little actual potato picking as possible. When the pickers to left and right of my stint had their backs turned I moved my stakes inwards by a yard or two. I also learned that it was quite easy to push many potatoes back into the loose soil with my boots. I even stooped to the despicable ploy of chatting-up the plump and plain girl on the next stint, then complaining of back pain to give her the opportunity to show how much she fancied me by picking on my stint as well as her own during most of the late afternoon. And despite all my wickedness I still earned half-a-crown.

These 18th century tallies recorded the landowner's name and a value of 1 shilling, expressed as 12 pence. They could be used for a wide range of crop picking activities - all to the value of 1 shilling. Their evolution from the medieval design is clear.

The coveted 120 bushel Kentish hop token. To earn one of these a family had to pick 960 gallons of hops.

Early 18th century hop token from Kent.

Dated hop tokens are rare. This example carries the date 1844.

Higher value agricultural tallies and tokens tend towards ornate lettering. The "B" for bushels on this specimen has elaborate flourishes.

Obverse and reverse of a 60 bushel token dating from 1847, and showing a representation of hops.

Not to scale

In Victorian times the hop factor's valuation of the crop determined how much each hop picking family received when they redeemed their hop tokens after the farmer had been paid by the factor.

Word got around in the evening that pickers on a neighbouring farm were earning five shillings a day. I made sure I arrived at that farm gate before 8am the next morning and soon found myself hired. Arrangements on the field seemed quite casual: no stakes marked our stints, and the farmer issued few orders. He just climbed into his tractor and began chugging up and down the rows. Suddenly I found myself knocked to the ground in the rush to get at the newly exposed spuds. Women almost clawed each other's eyes out when the tractor passed over a spot where the crop had grown heavily. And they guarded their filled sacks like female gorillas protecting young. I learned why about an hour later when a foreman came round with a low-loading trailer. For every full-to-the-brim sack he handed out a brass tally. I heard to my dismay that the pickers who had earned five shillings on the previous day had each filled 30 sacks. Late that evening I hobbled through the farm gate with just two-shilling-and-four-pence in my grubby palm.

The hop growers in Victorian Kent had a casual workforce that often topped 100,000 in a good season. The pickers, mostly Romany folk who had probably worked their way across Dorset, Hampshire and Sussex before arriving in time for Kentish cherries, then vegetables, then apples, then hops in September, lived in their caravans. But the 20,000 East and South London hoppers who poured into Kent every autumn often had to make do with rough shelters built from tarpaulins and sheep hurdles. They put up with the poor conditions because they needed the money. After a season of three or four weeks, an average family of man, wife and three youngsters, could expect to return to London with up to £20 in cash in addition to the new clothes and boots they bought on spending sprees in Kentish towns on the way home. But they only managed to accrue so much because the farmer paid in tokens until all of the crop had been harvested and sold. A few local shops accepted tokens for essentials such as bread and tea; whereas most local pubs displayed signs reading "No Dogs, Gypsies or Hoppers"; so most tokens remained un-cashed until the picking was all done.

Hops had been introduced into Kent in the 1500s, but the huge acreages requiring large numbers of casuals were not grown until the 19th century. Token needs up to about 1820 were probably met by the farmer, or a local blacksmith, casting lead in simple chalk moulds. A switch to lighter pewter tokens occurred before the middle of the 19th century, with a further switch to brass and copper after 1850. Commercial die-stampers had begun to supply farmers by that time, and a number of agriculturalists went to the expense of adding ornate touches to their designs, if only amounting to a flourish here and there on lettering and figures. The more adventurous minority had tokens made with eye-catching images such as Kentish prancing horses, oast houses, hares or family emblems and monograms.

Of course, pickers were much more concerned with the numbers stamped on hop tokens than with their designs. Several rather confusing numbering systems seem to have operated in Kent. There was a sequence than ran: 1, 2, 3, 4, 5, 6, 7, 8, 10, 11, 12, 15, 20, 25, 30, 50, 60, 100, and 120 Note that 9 was missed from the units as a safeguard against confusion - in the dusk at the end of a busy day - with an upside-down 6. The advantage of this system was that the tokens could be used to records shillings and pence, with 1 equal to a penny, and 30 equal to half-a-crown if used to tally other crops; or the same tokens could express bushels up to the largest 120-bushel load.

Another set ran: 1, 6, 12, 30, 60, 120, often with the word "bushels" following to make quite clear what was being measured. Each family of hoppers had a container with a capacity of I gallon. There were 2 gallons in a peck, and four pecks in a bushel; so the container had to be filled eight times to make a bushel. Little wonder that very few 120-bushel tokens come to light as finds by fieldwalkers. After filling their container 960 times to earn one of the highest value tokens, the family probably guarded it night and day. Nevertheless, such finds have been made.

A third set gave cash values of 1d, 6d, 1/-, 2/6d, and 5/-, but as the farmer never knew just how much the pickers would receive at payout time until the entire crops had been harvested and valued for quality by a wholesaler, these money-value tokens may have been used in other aspects of harvesting discussed below.

Although many hop tokens were die-cast in London and perhaps elsewhere after 1850, few makers have been identified. Only R. Neal of London and T.W. Richardson of Brede seem to have marked names or initials on their work for hop growers. Of course, the farmers usually identified themselves and farm names clearly to avoid having to pay for other farmers' labour. But when an owner moved to a new farm he often took his tokens with him, re-using them at that address without obliterating the old.

The majority of hop tokens were circular, although on some farms shape may also have aided identification, either of a farmer's own issues, or of a value in poor light when the number stamped upon it proved difficult to see. Square, triangular, octagonal, oval and lozenge shapes have been recorded. Although these tokens are strongly associated with Kent - East Kent most of all – hops were grown in Sussex, Herefordshire and Worcestershire, where tokens have also come to light. The Kentish finds have high collector appeal because accounts of hop picking in Kent have made us aware of the lives of the poor families to whom they represented hard

The ultimate destination of all hops. Numerous livelihoods depended on good hop harvests.

labour and hard cash. Many casuals from other towns and cities went into the countryside at harvest times to pick crops. At the time of my own exploits already mentioned, the local education authority designated a week in October as "Potato Picking Week". Schools closed and youngsters were expected to accompany parents on forays into the rural world to help with harvests. Counties such as Herefordshire and Devon required casual labour to pick apples as part of their cider-making cycle. The crop growers in the Home Counties whose produce fed Londoners - the soft fruit farms on Scotland's east coast and the salad horticulturalist in Lancashire - all took on extra hands at this time. To ensure they worked diligently, and stayed until the harvest was home, growers often relied on tallies and tokens rather than cash.

As explained in other chapters, the problem of obtaining small change was never properly tackled until the 1820s. Again, this goes some way to explaining why such rich crops of lead, copper and brass artefacts lie on so many arable fields.

Identifying Finds

Research on farm names, on farming family names, on crops grown in particular areas, even on local life during harvesting seasons when "foreigners" invaded the village, can all be carried out by amateur historians using internet resources and newspaper archives.

Recommended Further Reading

Hop Tokens Of Kent & Sussex by A.C. Henderson

Chapter 14

Control In The Workplace

Some 18th & 19th Century Industrial Uses For Tokens & Tallies

Pub landlords may have used the term "check" to mean a receipt for money handed over and pleasures paid for; but in an industrial context the word often implied some form of control over the workforce and its activities. It is necessary to bear in mind that the new factories and large-scale mining operations developed in the late 18th to early 19th century brought hundreds of men and women into restricting environments where each pair of hands had to perform certain tasks at certain times to ensure smooth running of the enterprise.

Crucial to that outcome was the physical attendance of each worker at the start of the working day; quite a change from the agricultural labourer's approach to time and his often irregular time-keeping in tune with the seasons of the year. What better way to ensure a man's/woman's presence than to issue each with a small disc stamped or otherwise impressed with his/her name or an allocated number, and to promulgate a rule that required presentation of the check to a gate-keeper at a fixed daily time to gain access to the place where wages could be earned?

In coal mining the process evolved into a check or token issuing system that not only recorded each miner's shift attendance, but also obliged him to register the issuing and return of his lamp with a second check. A benefit of the careful tallying to all concerned was that in the event of a serious accident (frequent occurrences in those days) the number of men who were working underground at the time could be accurately established.

In the pioneering days of large-scale coal and metal ore extraction these industries were often located in quite remote countryside with no access to shops and other urban facilities. Workers trudged several miles to get to the mine, and they faced even longer journeys into neighbouring towns to spend their wages. Philanthropic employers hit on the solution by opening company shops and stores close to the workplace where necessities could be purchased, sometimes at a lower price than in towns. But during periods of recession and low profitability, the temptation to use these outlets to generate additional income often proved too great. Unscrupulous bosses bought lightweight token coins from Birmingham back-street workshops and used them to pay wages. The worst offenders then hiked prices so that workmen fell into debt and thus became much less likely to go on strike. These cheating schemes became known as "truck" systems, perhaps in reference to the medieval *truck* meaning small wares or purchases. Officially outlawed in the 1830s, they nevertheless continued as bad practices in many factories and mines until the 1880s.

The pub checks discussed in the previous chapter occasionally became part of a truck fraud when a factory or mine owner bought a local pub and paid his men in checks that had to pass through the pub's till for purchases of beer, and for basic household goods

THE HARTON COAL COMPANY LIMITED
84
WORKMAN'S
RAILWAY
PASS
WHEN TRAVELLING
TO AND FROM
WORK
N.C.B.
316
STEETLEY UNIT
PILSLEY COLLIERY
SCHOOL
CHECK
2
D
BEWICKE MAIN COLLIERY
1811
ONE

Not to scale

Industrial Tokens & Tallies

Not to scale

Countermarked token showing signs of wear due to long years of circulation.

sold at a side-door. When a man's checks ran out he could obtain beer and basics on credit, driving him deeper into debt and more firmly into the boss' grip.

An inland mine with no immediate access to a navigable river faced the problem of getting its coal or ores into the hold of a ship for transportation to market. In many districts that need was met by teams of pack-mules carrying large wicker panniers into which loads were pitched by workers at the mine's surface. Recording the weights of coal or ore leaving the mine in this way generated a series of carriers' tokens, which the carrier had to hand in at the dockside.

It has already been demonstrated that mine and factory owners were among the most enthusiastic of token issuers. This was initially to alleviate their constant problem of where to find the small change to fill wage packets, but later to use the surfaces of tokens as advertising vehicles for their factories and business addresses. Within a few years tallies, checks and tokens in numerous forms pervaded most work places, controlling the issuing of raw materials and tools; recording the output of individual workers or shift teams; accounting for company property; measuring working time; and numerous other practices. Workers in different industries referred to tokens and tallies by various names – in coal mining they were "motties", "tickets", or "passes" – but they all amounted to the same rigorous methods of controlling workers at their places of employment. The various processes have left a wide range of tallies and tokens for today's collectors.

Identifying Finds In The Field

Any small piece of brass, copper, lead or aluminium bearing an impressed or incised number, or initial letters, or occasionally an image, found in the vicinity of an old mine, Victorian factory site, or long-abandoned quarry, is probably a relic of these practices.

Recommended Further Reading

Image of Industry – Coal by Thornes R., RCHM, 1994.

Terminology

I have included here only those abbreviations and technical terms likely to occur in dealers' descriptions, in catalogues, or on the surfaces of the sorts of tokens, tallies and other pieces covered by this book. Terms explained fully on previous pages are not repeated here; nor is this short list any substitute for the often-fuller definitions found in the recommended dictionaries mentioned at the end of the list.

Annulets: Doughnut-like rings, often seen between the arms of crosses on medieval tokens and hammered coinage.

B: Abbreviation for bushel.

Beaded: A line of raised dots, often forming a circle, around the borders of a piece, or surrounding part of the main decoration.

Blank Reverse: See "Uniface".

Bodle: Another name for the Scottish turner that circulated in England as a token farthing. Also known as a half-plack.

Bract: Abbreviation of bracteate.

Bracteate: A piece stamped on a thin metal flan with lettering, etc that shows through in reverse on the other side.

Bushel: A measure of capacity on agricultural tokens and tallies. One bushel equals 8 gallons dry capacity.

C/M or CTM: Abbreviations for countermarked, used in some catalogues.

Calendar: Seen on the reverses of some advertising tickets engraved with a multi-year calendar.

Cartouche: A frame, often ornate, surrounding some part of the design or lettering on a piece.

Casting Sprue: Waste lead/pewter/tin sometimes seen attached to edges of cast pieces.

Check: A receipt for payments or for goods/items/services that can be redeemed when the check is presented.

Counter: A gaming piece or a jetton with a value agreed between those who use it.

Countermarked: A mark stamped into an existing piece to alter its value, ownership or purpose.

Crenellated: Notches around edges of piece.

Cross Moline: a cross with broadened terminals.

Cut Corners: A square or oblong piece with its four corners cut off at 45 degrees.

Dozen: Often abbreviated to "D" on agricultural tokens, tallies and market checks. Not to be confused with the lower case "d" denoting pennies.

Edge Inscribed: Lettering cut into edge of piece during minting.

Exergue: The space, usually at the bottom, and beneath a main design, where a date, if any, normally appears.

Exonumia: The American (USA) equivalent of the British term paranumismatica.

Grained Edge: Another term for milled edge.

Incuse or Incised: Lettering, etc cut into surface of piece.

Inferior Issue: A lightweight imitation of a regal coin; often up to one-third lighter than the genuine coin.

Key Pattern: Ornate border like a series of key impressions.

Medalet: A coin-like piece, usually commemorating an event, person, or place and with a diameter of 25mm or less.

Mule: A piece with an obverse and a reverse not normally encountered together.

One Basket: Seen on market and farm tallies.

Pass: A piece to be presented when seeking admission.

Pierced: A hole formed during manufacture for hanging, etc.

Sack: The word occurs on tallies recording the hire of vermin-proof sacks for goods carried as early railway freight.

Sewn: Piece cast with holes for sewing to garments, etc.

Slotted: Elongated hole cut through piece for hanging or identification.

Spintriae: Roman tokens bearing (usually) pornographic images on obverse, with a numerical denomination of reverse. May have served as gaming tokens or for use in brothels.

Tag: A piece that identifies, prices or provides other information about the object to which it is/was attached.

Ticket: A piece on which no value is indicated, but which states the name, address and business details of the issuer, together with other information aimed at generating sales.

Uniface: Design, lettering, etc. on one side of piece only.

Voided: Shown in outline only (ie voided cross).

Recommended Further Reading

The Coin Encyclopaedia by Junge E. (Seaby).
The First Dictionary Of Paranumismatica by Edge B. (1991).

End Note

I said in the Introduction that the subject is vast and page space limited. Sadly I have exhausted page space long before exhausting the subject of tokens and tallies. But if what you have read and seen on the previous pages has whetted your appetite for more, I hope the books recommended as further reading will provide it, and that their reading lists will take you even further into the fascinating world of paranumismatics.

Make contact with the dealers and specialist collectors I have listed. They are mines of information and well-stocked to meet your collecting needs. If this book takes you in that direction I shall be more than satisfied, perhaps even encouraged to write a second volume to include what could not be squeezed into this one.

Ted Fletcher